The Starling

THE STARLING

A Biography

Stephen Moss

SQUARE PEG

1 3 5 7 9 10 8 6 4 2

Square Peg, an imprint of Vintage, is part of the Penguin Random House group of
companies whose addresses can be found at global.penguinrandomhouse.com

Penguin
Random House
UK

First published in the UK by Square Peg in 2024

penguin.co.uk/vintage

Typeset in 10/14.93 pt Dante MT Pro by Jouve (UK), Milton Keynes
Printed and bound in Latvia by Livonia Print

The authorised representative in the EEA is Penguin Random House Ireland,
Morrison Chambers, 32 Nassau Street, Dublin D02 YH68

A CIP catalogue record for this book is available from the British Library

ISBN 9781529908282

Penguin Random House is committed to a sustainable
future for our business, our readers and our planet. This book
is made from Forest Stewardship Council® certified paper.

To my long-time birding companion and dear
friend Graeme Mitchell, with whom I have
marvelled at many murmurations

Starling

We forget that you were once as common as coal,
Little coal-black bird.
Stumpy, dumpy. The wire-dotter, pylon-swarmer.
Camped out on our ledges and trees, screaming
England's towns down.
Noisy as a classroom on the last day of term.

We forget that you once shimmered through
frozen air; ripple bird.
Shape-shifter, dusk-dancer. Murmurer, sky-writer,
Endlessly becoming the darkening gold:
Animals, patterns, waves.
And how we, wonderstruck, witnessed a
 nightly unity against death . . .

Yet in the mad pursuit of a spotless life,
we believed you plague.
We forget that in loss it's the little things
that leave the largest holes . . .

We forget that you were once as common as coal,
And that fact makes your scarcity more keenly felt.
How losing you is devastating;
A hole both in sky and soul,
For it signifies a greater loss in us.

Rob Cowen

Contents

PROLOGUE

dusk breathes them in:
tens of thousands of starlings
streaming over reeds

John Barlow, *Wing Beats:*
British Birds in Haiku (2008)

The people come, first on their own, or in twos and threes, then in larger groups. As I walk alongside them I am reminded of a crowd heading to a football match, or a gathering of medieval pilgrims hoping to witness a miracle.

Both those analogies are strangely appropriate. It is, after all, just before three o'clock on a cold, bright, winter's afternoon, and for me at least, the fervour and intensity of this gathering does have something in common with the excitement and passion of football supporters, or a congregation of pious devotees awaiting a sign from God.

As we wait, flocks of teal – known as 'springs' from the way they launch themselves into the air as if fired by a gun – fly past on rapidly beating wings. They may be accompanied by other species of duck: gadwall, shoveler and wigeon, which have travelled here from Iceland, Scandinavia or even Siberia, just like the main attraction we are here to see.

Loose flocks of fieldfares and redwings – also winter visitors from the north and east – pass overhead, as do crows, jackdaws and pied wagtails, each seeking a place to spend the night in warmth and safety. Often these trigger a false alarm among the crowd: an excited response from some first-timers, quickly turning to muted embarrassment as they realise their faux pas.

There is usually a moment, around twenty minutes before sunset, when the gathering falls strangely silent, as if possessed of a shared appreciation of what we are about to witness. And then, just when some are beginning to wonder if they've come to the wrong place, or on the wrong day, the first birds appear in the far distance.

From here, without binoculars, they look like a puff of smoke, but a closer look reveals a small flock of starlings – a hundred or so – flying determinedly in our direction. A collective sigh of relief ripples through the crowd. We can relax.

The flock appears to be heading towards the reedbed that lies alongside the disused railway line giving us access into the RSPB's Ham Wall reserve, here on the Avalon Marshes in Somerset. But at the last moment it veers left, heads away and disappears over a distant line of trees. That initial sense of excitement rapidly becomes a sigh of frustration, as some people wonder, 'Is that really it?'

Fortunately, this was just the vanguard: a group of advance troops undertaking a swift recce to ensure they are in the right place. Moments later a second, this time much larger, flock arrives – then another, and another, until 10,000 or more birds are in the air at once.

And at last, as if triggered by a signal from an unseen leader, the main event begins. One flock suddenly tightens, and in doing so darkens, drawing our attention. As we watch, the birds collectively rise up into the air like a single, amoebous organism, twisting and turning to create transitory patterns which coalesce before disappearing almost as soon as they are formed.

Another flock joins the first, merging effortlessly, before this now much larger group drops towards the reedbed. Then, just as the birds appear to be going down, at the very last moment they change their minds and rise up again into the darkening sky.

The crowd reacts to each twist and turn with a mirrored response of

its own: a chorus of '*oohs*' and '*aahs*' like children witnessing a conjuror performing magic tricks. More birds come, and still more, until there must be at least 100,000 here. How on earth can we possibly know how many there are, asks someone. 'Just count the wings,' answers one wag in the crowd, 'and divide by two.'

Ten more minutes pass, though time appears to slow down. Now we enter a new phase in the proceedings: a large flock of latecomers, at least 5,000 strong, appears out of nowhere behind us, flying low over our heads.

And then we hear it: a soft, gentle sound like a giant whisper, made by the rushing of the starlings' wings as the air passes through them. It lasts for two or three seconds, and then is gone. It is this sound which gave rise to the collective name for a group of starlings: a murmuration. That is what we have travelled here – and gathered together in our own, equivalent human murmuration – to witness.

The numbers are reaching their peak: perhaps a quarter of a million individual birds. Still the flocks twist and turn, but now they are flying lower and lower, until they are just a few feet above the surface of the reeds, about to drop down to roost for the night. But there is one last, dramatic twist. Out of nowhere a female sparrowhawk appears, skimming fast and low over the reedbed on her broad, rounded wings.

The starlings respond instantaneously. As one, the flock rises higher and higher into the sky. But up here there is danger too: a male peregrine – the fastest creature on the planet – whose broad-based, triangular wings, short tail and deep chest all mark him out from other raptors. The peregrine folds his wings into his body to gain speed and shoots after one flock, hoping to grab one of the stragglers on the edge. Yet just as he is about to, the birds make one last, unpredictable aerial twist, somersaulting upwards en masse. Momentarily confused, the peregrine misses his target. His chance has gone: as the sun sets, the starlings are safe, and they start to land.

It is as if someone has pulled the plug out of a huge tank of water. The birds twist their wings to destabilise their flight pattern, and plummet randomly earthwards, streaming into the reedbed until you might think there was no more room to spare.

At the very moment when there are more birds perched than in flight, a manic chattering begins, almost as if the birds are discussing the near miss they have just experienced. The reeds themselves have turned from their usual buffish-brown shade to black, as though they have been singed by fire.

And still they come. Surprisingly large flocks of latecomers, which have travelled from farther afield than the earlier arrivals, from the coast at Bridgwater Bay at least, and probably much further. There is also the odd single individual, passing through the gloom without a care in the world – are these lone birds very brave, or simply very stupid, I wonder?

Ten minutes after sunset – only half an hour after it all began – the show is over. We can still hear the birds' unseen chattering, but the volume is dropping lower and lower, and they will soon fall silent. Those of us who have stayed for the whole event catch the eye of our fellow spectators and share a shy smile, acknowledging that we have experienced something very special; one that allows us, at least momentarily, to share that same sense of oneness as a football crowd or a religious congregation. As darkness falls we turn as one, and tramp back to the car park.

We are not the first, and will certainly not be the last, to enjoy that sense of a shared experience. Towards the end of the nineteenth century the naturalist and writer W. H. Hudson was already articulating our modern sense of wonder:

> At intervals . . . the whole vast concourse rises, and seen from a distance the flock, composed of tens and hundreds of thousands, may then be easily mistaken for a long black cloud . . . In a few minutes it is seen to

grow thin, as the flock scatters, until it almost fades away. Suddenly it darkens again; and so on, alternately, the form, too, changing continually, now extending to an immense length across the sky . . . and now gathered into a huge oval or oblong black mass; and by-and-by, the cloud again empties itself into the trees, and the sky is clear once more.

Artists and photographers, too, have been inspired by the visual spectacle of these birds. Since 2017 the Danish photographer Søren Solkær has travelled around Europe to capture striking images of the gatherings. He recalls being fascinated by seeing the murmurations as a child, growing up near the marshlands of southern Denmark. His photographs have been displayed in exhibitions, one called 'Black Sun', which refers to how the flocks seem to obscure the setting sun with darkness.

In his book of the same title Solkær provides an evocative explanation for his lifelong passion for the event:

The starlings move as one unified organism that vigorously opposes any outside threat. A strong visual expression is created – like that of an ink drawing or a calligraphic brush stroke – asserting itself against the sky . . . At times the flock seems to possess the cohesive power of super fluids, changing shape in an endless flux: from geometric to organic, from solid to fluid, from matter to ethereal, from reality to dream – an exchange in which real time ceases to exist and mythical time pervades. This is the moment I have attempted to capture – a fragment of eternity.

What can only be described as 'starling tourism' is not an entirely new phenomenon, but it has certainly spread in the past couple of decades, in part down to the impact of social media, which allows the posting – and easy viewing – of both amateur and professional footage of the murmurations. This in turn has led to people travelling long distances to see the remaining roosts, notably this one near my Somerset home, where on some winter weekend evenings there may be as many as 500 spectators gathering patiently to witness the event, some having travelled several hundred miles to be here. In response to this surge in visitor numbers, the RSPB has built a huge car park, and also a small visitor centre and toilets. It has even provided a 'Starling Hotline', enabling you to check out the latest location – helpful, as the birds tend to move around during the course of the winter, settling in different places as the season progresses.

Why we come to see them – and in such large numbers – is a trickier question to answer. After all, starlings have never been one of Britain's favourite birds. Indeed, they often evoke something closer to hostility than affection. Yet when they gather in such huge numbers, and especially when they perform their aerial acrobatics, we set negative feelings to one side and simply marvel at the sight we have been privileged to share. Few birds demonstrate the power of unity and co-operation better than starlings.

Maybe the reason we come is actually quite simple. Apart from a trip to a remote seabird colony – which can be tricky, time-consuming and sometimes stomach-churning – there are no natural spectacles in this country that we can experience on such a huge and impressive scale. At a time when, both as a society and as individuals, we are less and less in touch with the natural world, attending this fleeting but memorable event is a way we can reconnect, regain our primal sense of wonder – and still be home in time for tea.

As to why this has become such a popular event, I suppose it is something to do with the power and kinesis of the spectacle – a combination of ordered pattern and sheer anarchy as the birds create these momentary sculptures in the sky, wobbling and undulating like aerial amoebae, before finally settling in peace for the night.

Ironically, the increased interest in starlings has coincided with a rapid and worrying fall in their numbers. When I was growing up during the 1960s and 1970s, starling roosts were commonplace. Today, half a century or so later, not many remain. As well as this one on the Avalon Marshes, the best-known and most popular are at seaside locations, on Aberystwyth and Brighton piers. Other large and regular winter gatherings can be found at Gretna Green in the Scottish Borders, the Albert Bridge across the River Lagan in Belfast, and the RSPB reserves at Otmoor in Oxfordshire and Saltholme on Teesside. I've created a map of some of the best sites to see murmurations in the UK on page 14 to get you started. Smaller, sometimes more transitory ones can be also be found throughout lowland Britain, and there is even a 'Starling Murmurations Roost Map' available online, where you can check out sites near you and post details of new ones.

If you have never witnessed a starling murmuration – or only seen it on television or the World Wide Web – I strongly recommend you to. I have visited the Avalon Marshes roost well over a hundred times, yet I never tire of watching it. Some nights are better than others, of course, and if the birds do decide to go down in the far distance it can be frustrating. But that's the whole point of wildlife-watching – like a football fan watching yet another nil-nil draw, you have to suffer the dull days so that you really appreciate the great ones. And sometimes – just sometimes – the experience is simply unforgettable, even for an old hand like me.

In recent years many videos of starling murmurations have been shared with a wider audience. The YouTube video 'Murmuration' was filmed a decade or so ago by two young women, Liberty Smith and Sophie Windsor Clive, from a boat off the Irish coast. It has proved to be one of the most frequently shared of all the avian spectacles posted on this popular website, with over 11 million views. And they have also been celebrated in music. In 2013 the actor and singer-songwriter Johnny Flynn recorded 'Murmuration', which turns the image of a 'winged throng' of flocking starlings into a powerful and tender love song.

Yet as we shall discover, there is a lot more to the life of the starling than these winter gatherings. Indeed, I would argue that this is one of our most captivating birds, and certainly deserves a closer look. While researching and writing this book I have frequently been surprised at what I have learned – both about these birds' behaviour and about their (often ambiguous) place in our culture and history.

When it comes to starlings, the key word is 'sociable'. For unlike other, more territorial songbirds such as robins, wrens, thrushes and blackbirds, starlings often breed together in loose colonies, and frequently come together in flocks not just in the autumn and winter, but also during the breeding season.

Like the other five volumes in this series, *The Robin, The Wren, The Swallow, The Swan* and *The Owl, The Starling* aims to create a rounded portrait of this fascinating and much-maligned bird. As in the earlier books I have sought to combine the starling's biological life – its behaviour, ecology and so on – with its social and cultural one. Just as with my previous subjects, these two elements are closely interwoven: as I have discovered, the folklore about any bird is almost always derived from some specific aspect of its behaviour.

Being such a common and familiar bird – albeit rather more so in the past than today – the starling is inevitably part of our cultural lives. Its expert mimicry skills have tricked passers-by for centuries, from imitating the whistle of bombs during the Blitz to recreating the sound of our latest ringtones. These sophisticated linguistic talents have also made it invaluable to scientists. The starling's regular appearances in literature, music and popular culture run from the Celts and Romans via Chaucer, Shakespeare and Mozart to the huge Japanese media and gaming franchise Pokémon (in which one of the key characters, Starly, is based on an Asian species – probably the white-cheeked starling).

As this book seeks the truth about the starling it will debunk various oft-repeated myths. I will tell the story of the starling's success as a global species, achieved with a little help from, and sometimes in opposition to, us. And as with previous volumes, I devote a chapter to the close relatives of my main subject: a varied and truly fascinating family of birds.

I have once again drawn on the giants of ornithological literature who have gone before me: historical writers such as Thomas Bewick, John Clare and William MacGillivray, and more modern and contemporary authors and experts. For the latter, I have relied heavily on the renowned ornithologist and starling expert Dr Christopher Feare, whose 1984 monograph *The Starling* remains the most authoritative scientific account of the species.

I also include many of my own observations. Starlings have been a part of my life for as long as I can remember. From the suburban back garden where I grew up, in Shepperton on the outskirts of west London, via my many birding adventures up and down the country since, to the nightly winter murmurations I witness near my home on the Somerset Levels, I have always enjoyed watching starlings. They are not a bird you can easily get away from; nor would I ever want to.

So, whether you like and admire starlings, consider them a bit of a pest – or are somewhere in between – I hope you enjoy their story.

Starling Murmuration Sites

NOTE: Starling murmurations and roost sites are notoriously unpredictable. Some sites may be temporarily or permanently abandoned, or the birds might move a short distance away to a different location; also new sites appear from year to year!

ENGLAND

1. Blashford Lakes Nature Reserve, Ringwood, Hampshire BH24 3PJ: SU 151083
2. Brighton Pier, Brighton, East Sussex BN2 1TW: TQ 313038
3. Brockholes Nature Reserve, Lancashire PR5 0AG: SD 588306
4. East Chevington, Druridge Bay, Northumberland: NZ 270990
5. Exe Estuary, Countess Wear, Devon: SX 957885
6. Godmanchester Nature Reserve, Cambridgeshire PE29 2EJ: TL 264715
7. Ham Wall, Somerset BA6 9SX: ST 449396
8. Marbury Country Park, Cheshire CW9 6AT: SJ 561457
9. Otmoor Nature Reserve, Oxfordshire OX3 9TD: SP 570126
10. Potteric Carr, Yorkshire DN4 8DB: SE 588005
11. Redgrave and Lopham Fen, Diss, Suffolk IP22 2HX: TM 052802
12. Saltholme Nature Reserve, Middlesborough, Cleveland TS2 1TU: NZ 502231
13. Thameside Nature Discovery Park, Mucking, Essex SS17 0RN: TQ 685810

WALES

14. Newport Wetlands, Newport NP18 2BZ: ST351826

15. Royal Pier, Aberystwyth, Ceredigion SY23 2BH: SN 580818

16. Teifi Marshes, Pembrokeshire SA43 2TB: SN 187430

SCOTLAND

17. Brough, Thurso, Caithness KW14 8YE: ND 222733

18. Gretna Green, Dumfries & Galloway DG16 5HF: NY 310680

19. Mersehead Nature Reserve, Dumfries & Galloway DG2 8AH: NX 925562

NORTHERN IRELAND

20. Albert Bridge, River Lagan, Belfast BT7 2DS: NW 473293

Starling Fact Sheet	
Average size	Length 20–21 cm, wingspan 37–42 cm, weight 80 gm
Behaviour	Diurnal, sociable and very active, often gathering in flocks.
Range	Found in lowland and mid-altitude habitats throughout Britain and Ireland, including towns, cities, the countryside and offshore islands. Absent from most upland areas. More abundant in the east than the west.
Global Range	Common starlings can be found on every continent apart from Antarctica. They are native to Europe and Asia, and have been introduced to North America, parts of South America, and South Africa, Australia and New Zealand.
Breeding season in the UK	March to July
Eggs	4–6
Incubation period	12–15 days
Fledging period	19–21 days
Lifespan	Average 5 years (usually breeds after 2 years)
UK population	1.8 million breeding pairs; millions more come here from further north and east in autumn and winter.
Global population	Thought to be between 150 and 300 million individuals.

COMMON STARLING.
STURNUS VULGARIS.

I

INTRODUCTION TO STARLINGS

To most people he is a black bird, but to the cultivated
eye of the ornithologist he is much more.

W. Percival Westell, *British Bird Life* (1908)

Like most people, I tend to overlook starlings, especially when they are on their own or in small groups. But if I do stop for a moment, and take a closer look, I'm struck by what a remarkable bird this is. An individual starling exudes a quiet confidence, as if it at ease with itself, which I rather admire.

Yet we are so mesmerised by the sheer spectacle of those starling murmurations that it is very easy to overlook the bird itself. So let's take a closer look.

The common starling – whose scientific name *Sturnus vulgaris* translates as exactly that – is a fairly plump, short-tailed, medium-sized passerine (the group that makes up more than half of all the world's bird species). At 20–21 cm (about 8 inches) long, and weighing roughly 80 grams – less than 3 ounces – an adult starling is noticeably larger and heavier than a house sparrow, but slightly smaller, though marginally heavier, than a song thrush.

Whenever I see a starling, even in silhouette, I can always tell what it is. Whether on the ground or in flight, starlings appear rather stocky and well-built, with triangular wings, about twice as long as their rather short tail, and that distinctive long, pointed bill; overall, their appearance has an almost gothic feel.

In autumn and winter, when starlings moult into their non-breeding

plumage, their breast, belly and back are flecked with small white markings – is it perhaps too fanciful to wonder if these star-like speckles gave the bird its name? But in spring and summer these are far less prominent, because as the bird's feathers begin to wear, these paler markings are harder to see. Whenever I see starlings at this time of year I am struck by their smoother, glossier, darker and more iridescent hue – not quite as impressive as the glossy starlings I have seen in Africa, but very handsome, nonetheless.

If I am watching from a distance, or in poor light, starlings do appear very dark – indeed, almost black, as the popular Edwardian nature writer W. Percival Westell astutely observed. But when I get closer I can usually see an almost metallic sheen on their plumage. Especially when the bird turns to face towards the light, shades of purple, green and brown are reflected back at me, like a wafer-thin layer of oil across a puddle.

In spring and summer an adult starling's legs are a striking bubble-gum pink (they turn brownish in autumn and winter), while the bill is a custard yellow, fading to a very dark brown outside the breeding season. And although I have to look quite hard to see this, during the spring and summer the base of the male's bill turns a subtle shade of pale blue, while that of the female is an even paler pink.

The species' other name, European starling, reflects the fact that it breeds across virtually the whole of mainland Europe, from well inside the Arctic Circle, at Varangerfjord in the far north of Norway, all the way south to Greece – with the notable exception of most of the

Iberian Peninsula, where it is replaced by its close relative the spotless starling (see page 29).

Starlings also breed from the Azores in the west, in the coastal regions of North Africa, and further eastwards, across much of central Asia, to Pakistan, India, Nepal and Mongolia. In the milder southern and western parts of the species' European range they are mainly sedentary. But like other songbird species, birds breeding farther north and east head south-west in late summer and autumn, to places with a more benevolent winter climate – including the British Isles.

The starling has been introduced – sometimes accidentally, but often quite deliberately – from its native home in Europe and western Asia to many other parts of the world. It can now be found in Australia and New Zealand, South Africa, the Pacific island nation of Fiji and, most notoriously of all, North America, where it has become a major agricultural pest.

The starling's large natural range, together with those non-native birds' success in colonising very different climatic zones, shows just how adaptable it is. Only the house sparrow rivals the starling in its ability not just to survive, but thrive, in such a wide array of geographical locations around the world.

This adaptability might serve the starling well in the future, as *A Climatic Atlas of European Breeding Birds* (2007) reveals. The authors' computer modelling for the effects of the climate crisis suggests that in future the starling might no longer be able to breed successfully in the southernmost parts of its European range, owing to much hotter and drier summers. However, it is likely to be able to colonise new regions as far north as Svalbard. At a latitude of 78 degrees North, this is as far away from London as Western Sahara is to the south. However, this modelling does not consider the potentially negative effects of climate change across the central part of the starling's range – especially summer droughts, which can dramatically reduce the food available for both breeding birds and their offspring.

The key reason for the success of our starling, both in its natural range and in places where it has been introduced, was an ancestral change in diet, which led to the species being able to exploit a far wider range of habitats and geographical locations than its ancestors.

Many other members of its family – especially those living in tropical forests – have a far more specialised diet, feeding mainly on fruit. This has led to a largely arboreal existence: these birds spend most of their lives in trees. However, at some point in the family's evolutionary history, one of the common starling's ancestors dropped down to the ground, and began feeding on insects and other invertebrates, as well as on fruits and berries.

This more varied diet in turn led to major changes in the bird's anatomy and morphology: its form and body structure. Of these perhaps the most important factor in the species' future success was the bill, which became larger and stronger, to enable the starling to probe deeper into the ground and feed on insects and other soil-dwelling invertebrates.

A further advantage to this new diet was that starlings could continue to feed on dormant invertebrates during the autumn and winter months. Unlike other insectivorous birds such as swallows, warblers and flycatchers, which must head south in autumn when food becomes scarce, they were now able to stay put, rather than risking a long and arduous migration.

This allowed the species to spread westwards, into the temperate regions of western Asia and Europe. And, as the migration scientist Peter Berthold has pointed out, it also meant that as a largely resident species the common starling could start nesting earlier than its

migratory counterparts and, across much of its range, raise two broods of young each breeding season.

However, the biggest factor in the starling's expansion of range and rise in numbers, just as with the house sparrow, was a seismic change in human behaviour 12,000 years or so ago. From a previously nomadic, hunter-gatherer existence, there was a wholesale switch to a more settled way of life, facilitated by the cultivation of crops and the domestication of livestock.

Over the next few millennia those early farmers cut down woods and forests and built permanent settlements – what would eventually become the same villages, towns and cities where the starling lives alongside us today. Our homes, barns and other buildings provided new opportunities for the birds to make their nests; meanwhile, the growing and harvesting of crops such as wheat and barley, and the raising of farm animals such as cattle, sheep and pigs, delivered two abundant new sources of food, in the form of spilt grain and insects.

Today, when we watch a flock of starlings marching across a grassy

field like a conquering army, we are witnessing a relatively recent change in the species' behaviour. This is also what ultimately led to their global success. As Chris Feare concludes, the main beneficiary from this historic change was not us, but the starling:

> Man and his agriculture have . . . clearly been instrumental in opening up a large area of the globe to the starling, and the relationship between these two species has been close . . . I described this relationship as commensal, rather than symbiotic, [although] we shall see that the relationship does tend to favour the starling at man's expense.

Like many other globally common and widespread species, the common starling has evolved into a dozen different races (subspecies), each of which varies slightly in plumage and measurements from the others. These are mostly found on the outer limits of the starling's range, including the Faroe Islands in the north, the Azores in the west, and Crimea, eastern Turkey, Afghanistan, Kashmir, Nepal and Pakistan to the east.

The nominate race we see in Britain, *Sturnus vulgaris vulgaris*, is by far the most common and widespread, and found throughout most of Europe. This includes Iceland (where it started breeding as recently as the mid-1930s, and is one of a handful of breeding songbirds), and the Canary Islands.

From a British viewpoint, the most familiar race (apart from *vulgaris*) is the subspecies *zetlandicus*, found on the Shetland Isles. I have watched flocks of these birds in midsummer, at the ancient settlement of Jarlshof, towards the southern end of the Shetland archipelago. Here, as in the rest of the Northern and Western Isles, starlings nest not in trees, but in nooks and crannies, including the grey stone walls of its ancient, ruined buildings, for reasons noted in *The Handbook of British Birds* (1940):

> Owing to absence of trees, breeds usually in recesses in sea-cliffs, also under boulders on shore, holes in walls of any kind and frequently in rabbit, rat or other holes in ground, as well as in stone heaps and peat stacks.

Their secretive nesting behaviour also differs from the brash, noisy starlings on the mainland, according to a note in *British Birds* magazine by Donald Cross, mentioned by David Bannerman in his epic, twelve-volume *The Birds of the British Isles* (1953):

> Another noteworthy characteristic of Shetland starlings is the way they avoid showing themselves during laying and incubation . . . Prior to hatching, Mr Cross states that it is possible to watch a particular inlet

in the cliffs where a dozen or more pairs are known to be nesting, and to see no sign of any birds even after watching the entrance holes for hours.

While the adults of the Shetland race appear very similar to the ones we see on the British mainland (although they do have slightly longer wings and a broader bill), the youngsters I saw looked very different to me: they were noticeably darker in colour, and indeed at a distance appeared almost black.

Starlings found on nearby Fair Isle, located halfway between Shetland and Orkney, and also those on the Hebrides appear to be intermediate between the Shetland and nominate races – the young are also very dark compared with birds on the British mainland – and may possibly have originally evolved as hybrids between the two.

Apart from the common starling, only two other members of its large and varied family are found in Europe. As both its English and scientific names suggest, the spotless starling, *Sturnus unicolor*, lacks its commoner cousin's white spots, and remains a dark, glossy colour all year round. It also has longer feathers on its throat, which are surprisingly noticeable when the male sings.

The spotless starling has a very restricted world range, centred on the western Mediterranean, with its main strongholds in Spain, Portugal and north-west Africa. It can also be seen on the islands of Corsica, Sardinia and Sicily, yet not, oddly, the Balearic Islands, which lie in between these two regions.

Since the early 1980s (soon after the common starling spread westwards into the Iberian peninsula, so the ranges of the two species now overlap) the spotless starling has also spread slowly north-eastwards, into the far south-west corner of mainland France. On a visit there a decade or so ago, I watched a small flock of these birds feeding beside the beach, at a holiday resort on the Med. At first I thought they were just common starlings, but as they took off the glossy, almost-black appearance was obvious.

In February 1998, a vagrant spotless starling was reported from the Isles of Scilly, initially attracting hordes of excited twitchers keen to bag what would have been the very first record for Britain. To their dismay and frustration, however, a close analysis of photographs suggested that the bird was simply an unusually dark and rather glossy common starling, lacking the usual white spots.

To date, therefore, this species has not officially occurred in the wild in Britain, although it has since been claimed (also unsuccessfully) in the Netherlands. And unlike other species such as egrets and even bee-eaters, which have rapidly shifted their range north as a result of climate change, the spotless starling is very sedentary in its habits, so is likely to stay put.

That certainly doesn't apply to the other European species, the rosy (or rose-coloured) starling, which is far more nomadic. As its name suggests, the adult rosy starling is a strikingly attractive bird, with a pale pink breast, belly and mantle, strongly contrasting with its dark head, neck, wings and tail. Juvenile birds are similar to, although noticeably paler than, young common starlings. Incidentally, older bird books often refer to the species as the 'rosy pastor', from the scientific name *Pastor roseus* – presumably a reference to its habit of feeding alongside sheep. This distinctive species is a characteristic breeding bird of the plains of eastern Europe, and the wide-open grassy steppes of west and central Asia, where it nests in huge colonies, sometimes numbering in the tens of thousands.

The rosy starling's colonial breeding habits have led to it being encouraged as a natural pest controller, especially in China's north-western

province of Xinjiang, to try to reduce the use of expensive and polluting insecticides. The birds were helped by the provision of artificial nests, but ironically so many starlings flocked to the area that there were no longer enough locusts for the birds to feed on, and whole broods of young starlings died even before fledging.

Rosy starlings generally migrate south and east, to spend the winter months in Arabia and India. However, this is what scientists call an irruptive species, which means that after the breeding season is over, in mid-to-late summer, the birds are prone to long-distance wanderings in search of food. This may bring them westwards towards our shores, where they often join forces with flocks of their commoner relative.

Surprisingly, perhaps, the first British record of rosy starlings was in London, some time in the early decades of the eighteenth century. Shot in Norwood (it is not clear whether this is the district of south London or the one near Ealing), the bird was stuffed and then put on display for customers of a Chelsea coffee house. In the two centuries

since then, there have been only another ten London records of this scarce and attractive species.

Although rosy starlings usually arrive in Britain during late summer or early autumn, they do sometimes stay around for longer. A couple of Christmases ago I headed over to the village of Wiveliscombe in west Somerset, where a juvenile rosy starling – just beginning to moult into its adult garb, and so looking rather tatty – had been present for a week or so. It perched, incongruously, on solar panels covering the roof of a modern house at the edge of the village, and gave me brief but good views, before it flew off to feed with a flock of common starlings.

Few British birds are quite as paradoxical as the starling. The bird itself is not necessarily contradictory, but our attitudes towards it certainly are. As Bill Oddie wryly observed, while waiting for a huge murmuration of starlings to come to roost, the starling is probably not most people's favourite bird . . . a bit of a bully on the bird table, always squitting on precious government buildings and, be honest, not the most mellifluous of singers . . .

Typically, of course, Bill was playing devil's advocate; he actually loves and admires starlings. As does Chris Feare, who freely confesses in his monograph, *The Starling*, that he considers the starling to be 'beautiful'; yet at the same time quotes an unnamed friend who described it as 'the second-hand car salesman of the bird world'.

Others see the starling as the avian equivalent of a loudmouthed spiv, a football hooligan or, as Bill Oddie alluded, a bird-table bully. That verdict certainly chimes with what many people feel when a large flock of these brash, noisy birds suddenly materialises outside their kitchen window, scaring all the smaller species away.

Such a negative reputation is the fate of many common and widespread birds, especially those that, like starlings, tend to gather in large, noisy flocks. Perhaps this is because we find them disturbing and (as in Daphne du Maurier's short story and Alfred Hitchcock's film *The Birds*) even rather frightening. At the turn of the nineteenth century, the engraver and author Thomas Bewick was commenting on the species' ubiquity:

Few birds are more generally known than the starling, it being an inhabitant of almost every climate; and as it is easily trained in a state of captivity, its habits have been more frequently observed than those of most other birds.

In North America, where the starling is now also ubiquitous, the authors of the seminal *A History of North American Birds* describe it as 'handsome in plumage and of graceful shape'. However, a closer look reveals that the book was first published in 1874, and only included the starling because it was an 'occasional and rare visitant to Greenland'. Having been introduced to North America soon afterwards (see Chapter 6), nowadays starlings often provoke hostility, and have been roundly condemned as 'destructive interlopers from across the pond'. As in Britain, they have also been killed in huge numbers in (often fruitless) attempts to protect crops and livestock production.

Yet this species was not always regarded in quite such an unfavourable light. William Yarrell and William MacGillivray – two nineteenth-century ornithologists who agreed on very little else – both praised the starling, MacGillivray indeed describing it as 'one of our most beautiful native birds', while Yarrell was even more effusive: 'The starling is one of our handsomest birds . . . intelligent and sprightly, with a retentive memory, and great flexibility of voice.'

In *The Birds of Somersetshire* (1869), Cecil Smith perceptively pointed out that our response to the starling tends to depend on how good a view we get:

> The starling is a beautiful bird when seen close, in consequence of the glossy metallic tints with which its whole plumage is shot, though at a little distance it appears to be a dark, commonplace-looking bird.

But it takes a poet's eye to truly capture the quirky combination of characteristics that turns the starling from just another 'little brown job' into an object of real beauty. The twentieth-century Scottish poet Norman MacCaig, whose rare combination of acute observation and forensically accurate language made him a worthy successor to John Clare, wrote frequently about starlings.

MacCaig's concentration on particular aspects of their appearance, movement or behaviour leads him in 'Starlings', written in 1967, to compare them to 'a congregation of mediaeval scholars quarrelling in several languages', while in his 1980 poem 'Starling on a Green Lawn' he notes how the colour of their plumage alters as they move in relation to the light:

> He angles himself to the sun and his blackness
> Becomes something fallen from a stained-glass window.

But what captivated MacCaig most about starlings was their movement: that jaunty jerkiness as the bird moves systematically across the short turf of a park or garden lawn in search of food:

> He makes such a business of going somewhere
> he's like a hopping with a bird in it.

Its movement is certainly one of the starling's most distinctive characteristics, whether on the ground or in the air, as the ornithologist Bernard Tucker notes so precisely in *The Handbook*:

> On ground bustling activity and quick, jerky walk are characteristic; also runs and, less frequently, hops. Flight swift and direct, with rapidly moving wings . . . varied by glides with wings extended; but when hawking for high-flying insects adopts distinct wheeling and gliding action recalling swallow.

Sadly, birders often ignore starlings, at least away from those memorable murmurations. It is all too easy to focus on rarer and more obviously exciting birds, like avocets or ospreys, while overlooking the

commoner ones – those we come across almost every day. I am certainly as guilty of this as anyone.

And few British birds are quite as ubiquitous, throughout the year, as the starling. That's because, rather like our commonest British bird, the wren, they are not at all fussy about where they live, as the authors of *The Handbook* also noted: 'Catholic in choice of haunts, frequenting town and country, cultivated and uncultivated ground, and even treeless islands.' Starlings can be found in urban parks as well as rural fields, on open moors and coastal beaches, and – like other adaptable species such as crows and gulls – frequently feeding on landfill sites. Few people, if any, have never seen a starling.

The meanings of the names of many common birds – including all but one of the subjects of my 'bird biographies' – are something of a mystery. 'Owl' is clearly onomatopoeic, based on the male tawny owl's

hooting call, while 'robin' is a relatively modern human nickname added to the original name of 'redbreast'. But the origin of the names 'wren', 'swallow' and 'swan' are a puzzle to modern linguists, as is the word 'starling'. According to the *Oxford English Dictionary* it first appeared in written English around the year 1325, but actually goes back many centuries before then, to the Anglo-Saxon 'stærling'.

The doyen of bird name studies, the late Professor W. B. Lockwood of the University of Reading, explained that the bird's original Old English name was 'stare', which in turn derived from the Latin *sturnus* – from an unknown Indo-European root meaning 'starling' (which doesn't really help us with what the word might actually *mean*). We can tell this name is very ancient, as (with minor changes in spelling) it is still used as the name of this species in Norwegian, Swedish, Danish and German, though not, rather oddly, in Dutch, where it is called the *spreeuw*.

Professor Lockwood went on to explain that 'starling' – which dates back in English to well before the Norman Conquest – is in fact a more recent diminutive, referring to the bird's offspring, as in other common words for young or baby birds: 'duckling' and 'gosling'. As the US linguist

Arika Okrent wrote in 2013, 'Is there any suffix more adorable than the lovely little -ling? It gives us yearlings and starlings, downy ducklings and goslings, affectionate darlings and siblings, and comforting tender dumplings.' I wonder if the use of the diminutive in the name 'starling' – together, perhaps, with the sociable nature of the bird itself, and its ubiquity and familiarity – might also be the reason for its presence in the names of characters and the titles of books in popular culture.

A quick search on Amazon for book titles with the word 'starling' produces a surprising profusion, especially in books aimed at children and young adults. But by far the best-known use of the name 'Starling' for a fictional character is the protagonist of Thomas Harris's 1988 book *The Silence of the Lambs*, Clarice Starling. Played in the 1991 film by Jodie Foster, Clarice is a young and superficially naïve FBI trainee who is assigned the role of interviewing the psychopathic and cannibalistic serial killer Dr Hannibal Lecter, played by Anthony Hopkins.

The resultant stand-off between the two characters contains some of the most memorable dialogue of any Hollywood movie, and rightly won Oscars for both Hopkins and Foster. At one point, Lecter relentlessly probes Clarice about her family background and low social class:

> Good nutrition has given you some length of bone, but you're not more than one generation from poor white trash, are you, Agent Starling? And that accent you've tried so desperately to shed? Pure West Virginia.

Here, it seems to me, is why Thomas Harris chose this unusual surname in the first place: it perfectly fits the character of Clarice. Just as 'common' starlings are outsiders and outcasts in North America, so is she.

Over time, the original name 'stare' was superseded by the diminutive 'starling', which by then had lost its original sense of referring to the young birds. By the time William Turner published his 1544 work *Avium praecipuarum* (the first printed book devoted wholly to birds), 'starling' was the only form he used: for the adults as well as for the youngsters.

However, the original name appears to have lasted far longer in Ireland. W. B. Yeats's poem 'The Stare's Nest By My Window', published a century ago in 1924, opens with a precisely observed account of a starling's nest, built in a hole in a crumbling wall:

> The bees build in the crevices
> Of loosening masonry, and there
> The mother birds bring grubs and flies.
> My wall is loosening, honey bees
> Come build in the empty house of the stare.

The image of 'the empty house of the stare', repeated at the end of each of the four short verses, is a striking metaphor for Ireland's broken society, reinforcing the poem's subtitle, 'Meditations in the Time of Civil War'. Whether or not 'stare' was still in use for the starling in Ireland at the time, or Yeats's usage was deliberately archaic, the poet was clearly aware of the bird's original name.

Other common names for the species include 'starnel', preferred by John Clare in his 1827 poetry collection *The Shepherd's Calendar*:

> Blackening through the evening sky
> In clouds the starnels daily fly
> To Whittlesea's reed-wooded mere . . .

W. B. Lockwood claimed that the name 'starnel' was still occasionally heard in northern and eastern England well into the late twentieth century; I would be fascinated to hear from readers whether it is still in use there nowadays.

The species also has a plethora of folk names. Some, such as 'starnil' and 'starn', are simply a variation on the original; others, including 'black starling' and 'black steer', referring to the bird's apparent dark colour when viewed at a distance. Francesca Greenoak, in her fascinating collection of folk names *All the Birds of the Air* (1979), noted that because starlings frequently perch on the backs of sheep to pick off ticks, the species was also known as the 'sheep stare' (in Somerset), the 'sheeprack' (Northamptonshire) and the 'shepster' or 'sheppie' (Cheshire). In his epic two-volume *Thesaurus of Bird Names* (1998), Michel Desfayes listed at least 40 English folk names, including several with the prefix 'gyp' (meaning dark or black, as in 'gypsy'), such as 'gyp-starnel', along with 'star-thrush', 'jester-bird' and, my favourite (from Norfolk), 'chimney-pot plover' – from the bird's frequent habit of perching on chimneys.

However, I take issue with Desfayes' claim that 'starlings do not usually associate with sheep or any other animals,' and that therefore those sheep-related names merely 'imply the notion of flocking, a characteristic of the bird'. As Cecil Smith observed in Somerset, more than a century earlier:

> The starling is . . . very fond of feeding on ticks and other parasitical insects which are to be found in sheep's wool, and may often be seen enjoying a quiet ride on a sheep's back and at the same time getting a very good dinner.

The common starling is just one of almost 120 extant species (plus several now sadly extinct ones) in the family Sturnidae: the starlings and mynas. This Old-World group of birds is widely distributed across much of temperate and tropical Europe, Africa and Asia, extending to islands in the western Pacific, with one species, the glossy-green metallic (or shining) starling, even reaching the far north and east of Australia. Starlings and mynas are most closely related to the New World family Mimidae, the thrashers and mockingbirds, which, as both their English and scientific names suggest, are also excellent mimics.

Another group, Buphagidae – the oxpeckers, two African species which are famed for feeding on the backs of large game animals – were for a long time included in the starling family, but have now been separated following comparative analysis of their DNA.

Starlings also bear a superficial resemblance to another large, noisy and diverse family of birds in the New World: the icterids or New World blackbirds (of the family Icteridae). This includes orioles, meadowlarks, grackles, cowbirds, oropendolas and caciques, as well as the New World 'blackbirds'. However, the similarities between the two families are merely superficial, a result of convergent evolution, when they each learned to exploit similar grassland and forest-edge habitats.

Starlings and mynas share a number of qualities which, although not unique to this group, are very distinctive. They are medium-sized passerines, often quite robust in build, with slender (and often slightly downcurved) bills, stout legs, short tails and pointed wings. Some species – especially the African glossy-starlings – have distinctive coloured eyes, the irises often a bright shade of red, yellow or orange (or sometimes pale white), probably because this helps the birds signal to others in their flock.

They are mostly fairly dark, though some species, notably the golden-breasted and superb starlings, are very brightly coloured. As with our own starling, many species have either a glossy plumage, or patches of iridescence which shine when turned towards the light.

Because these patches are more visible to the birds themselves, whose eyes are far more sensitive than ours to ultraviolet light, they may help to influence a choice of mates.

Starlings and mynas tend to be sociable birds, with some breeding in colonies (or loose colonies). Many species build their nest in holes and cavities, either in trees, rocks or man-made buildings, and most are monogamous.

That sociability often continues outside the breeding season, with the birds gathering together in large feeding flocks or, in the case of the common starling, those huge nightly gatherings at their winter roosts. Other species – especially those living on the African savannah – are nomadic, moving around from season to season in response to shifts in weather and climate in order to find food, such as vast flocks of swarming locusts. That ability to travel – and to adapt rapidly to new homes – undoubtedly led to the group's success in colonising other parts of the globe, either naturally or with a helping hand from us.

Of all the members of this large and diverse family, our own familiar starling is easily the most abundant, and also has by far the largest geographical range. Indeed, with a total population thought to number between 150 and 300 million individuals – probably closer to the top end of that estimate – it is well inside the top ten of the most abundant species of wild bird on the planet.

The common starling aside, starlings and mynas are mostly found in two of the world's biogeographical regions. These are the Sino-Indian, which extends across the Indian sub-continent and South-east Asia, and the Afrotropical, which covers sub-Saharan Africa. By far the highest diversity occurs in East Africa, where more than twenty different species can be found, although some of these are very rare and localised. Within these regions they have evolved to exploit a wide range of habitats. They can be found in woods and forests, from sea level to the foothills of the Himalayas; open steppes, grasslands and savannah; forest edge and riverine habitats; and even a number of oceanic islands in the remote parts of the Pacific Ocean.

One of my favourite species, Tristram's starling, is named after the Victorian clergyman and ornithologist Henry Baker Tristram (and is also known, erroneously, as Tristram's grackle). This is a familiar bird of the deserts of the Middle East, found from Israel and Jordan in the north to Saudi Arabia and Yemen in the south. Glossy black in appearance, when the birds take to the air they reveal prominent rusty-orange patches on their wings. Birders visiting the region for the first time are often surprised to see large flocks of this sociable, noisy bird at service stations, where they gather to steal food from unwary picknickers while uttering their famous 'wolf-whistle' calls, vaguely reminiscent of the song of the golden oriole.

Yet even the most common and widespread species, such as the greater blue-eared, splendid and violet-backed starlings, have a very small range compared with the common starling, whose world distribution is larger than any other species by far, covering roughly 30 per cent of the Earth's land surface (excluding Antarctica). This has led Chris Feare to dub *Sturnus vulgaris* both 'the adaptable starling', and 'the successful starling'.

I shall go into more detail about the other species of starlings – and mynas – in Chapter 6. These comprise some of the world's most striking and fascinating birds, including a score or more of the glossy-starlings, large, and often long-tailed, and among the commonest and most recognisable residents of the African plains.

But there are also some very rare and localised species, such as the Socotra starling, found only on its eponymous island in the Arabian Sea, and the Bali starling (or myna). This striking bird once had the unenviable distinction of being considered the rarest bird in the world, due to its very limited rage on the island of Bali, its illegal capture as a status symbol within Indonesia and high value in the international bird trade. Fortunately it has now been brought back from the brink of extinction.

Two species of myna, the common (or Indian) myna and its close relative the common hill myna, have both become popular cage birds, due to their uncanny ability to mimic the human voice. The common myna also rivals the common starling as an invasive pest species in many parts of the world.

Each of these species has a fascinating story to tell. But before I do so, I shall trace the life cycle of our own familiar starling, alongside its historical, cultural and literary representations, through the four seasons of the year. I begin in my own garden, on the edge of the Somerset Levels, one New Year's Day.

STARLING.

Sturnus vulgaris, *Linn.*
Winter.

Litho. W. Greve, Berlin.

2

WINTER INTO SPRING

The starling sings more or less all of the year, but his song is at its best during the spring months. He has no such melodious notes as distinguish the warblers; his merit lies less in the quality of the sounds he utters than in their endless variety.

W. H. Hudson, *British Birds* (1895)

That New Year's Day I woke up with a pounding hangover. The night before I had overindulged at a celebratory dinner with friends, before staying over at their home in a nearby village. As I staggered outdoors bleary-eyed just after dawn, the very first bird I saw was a starling – not just one, moreover, but a small flock passing overhead, like dark punctuation marks against the slowly lightening sky. Having left their reedbed roost on the Avalon Marshes, they were now spreading out across the flatlands of Somerset, to feed in the flooded fields and farmyards nearby.

Soon afterwards we headed home ourselves. Feeling a little better, I spent the next half an hour or so in the back garden, indulging in my regular new year ritual of starting my annual bird list. Here the first bird was a house sparrow, chirping cheerily from the tiled roof of our house. He was almost immediately accompanied by the rapid song of an unseen wren from the hedgerow, and soon followed by a close-up view of a robin, delivering his more tuneful melody from the top branch of an elder.

The usual crew then began to arrive: a collared dove on our neighbours' roof, and a trio of corvids overhead – carrion crow and rook, of course, but also the larger and more impressive raven; once rare, but now a common sight in these parts. These were swiftly accompanied by a flock of wintering redwings (all the way from Iceland) flying over-head, a blackbird delivering his distinctive alarm call in the shrubbery, and a bright male chaffinch, adding a welcome flash of deep rose-pink to the dull, grey winter scene. All more or less what I would expect – especially now the wren has joined the robin in the small and exclusive group of birds that sing regularly during the winter months, to defend their territory.

But then, as I shivered in the January chill, and was just about to head indoors for a cup of coffee, I heard a song I didn't expect to hear: that of a starling. I say 'song', but the word does not quite do justice to the bizarre sound I was listening to. When W. H. Hudson emphasises the starling song's 'endless variety', rather than its tunefulness, he is spot-on.

What I could hear, on that opening day of the new year, was an out-pouring of rattles, whistles, warbles and buzzes, interspersed with another strange sound, which reminded me of one from my child-hood. That was the weird unmusical noise I used to hear coming from my analogue radio as I tried – usually unsuccessfully – to tune into the pop-music station Radio Luxembourg beneath the bedclothes, hoping my mother didn't realise I was still awake so long after bedtime.

As Hudson goes on to explain:

> In a leisurely way he will sometimes ramble on for an hour, whistling and warbling very agreeably, mingling his finer notes with chatterings and cluckings and squealings, and sounds as of snapping the fingers and of kissing, with many others quite indescribable.

A later writer, the ornithologist Kenneth Williamson, described the starling's song as 'the one-man band of the bird world, with no particu-lar tune to play', which sums it up rather well.

I suppose this is what we might expect from this paradoxical bird, which seemingly refuses to bend to convention in every aspect of its life. Instead of falling in line with its fellow songbirds and producing something that at least *attempts* to impersonate a tune, it goes its own way. The starling's song reminds me of listening to a frenzied jazz musician, continually improvising, ad-libbing and experimenting until you might imagine there are no more notes and phrases left to play. The phrase 'marvellous discords' has been used to describe the sound of a flock of glossy starlings, and also applies to our own familiar species. Again, Bernard Tucker summed up the song's unique qualities in his brilliantly concise yet perfectly accurate description in *The Handbook*:

> A lively rambling medley of throaty warbling, chirruping, clicking, and gurgling sounds, interspersed with mystical whistles and pervaded by a peculiar creaky quality.

The starling performing in my garden that New Year's Day was singing a few weeks earlier than usual, at least in these parts. A glance at my bird notes over the years shows that a more typical date for me to hear the first starling song is some time between late January and early February. Maybe this one was simply an outlier among his tribe, or perhaps, like so many other songbirds, starlings are now starting to sing earlier than they used to, as a result of our springs shifting earlier, prompted by the effects of climate change. Either way, it was a surprise – and a pleasure – to hear him.

I am not the only listener to have found the starling's song strangely compelling. In March 1668 the celebrated diarist Samuel Pepys wrote approvingly of 'a starling which . . . doth whistle and talk the most and

best that ever I heard anything in my life'. The composer Wolfgang Amadeus Mozart was another early admirer, keeping a starling as a pet for over three years. Indeed, so attached did he become to the bird that when it died, in June 1787, he held a funeral procession in its honour, reading a verse requiem, before burying it in his garden in Vienna. The German-American academic Robert Spaethling translated the composer's funeral verse into English, proving without doubt that Mozart was a better composer than he was poet:

> Here rests a bird called Starling,
> A foolish little Darling.
> He was still in his prime
> When he ran out of time,
> And my sweet little friend
> Came to a bitter end,
> Creating a terrible smart
> Deep in my heart.

It has been suggested that Mozart's pet starling inspired him to write the theme to his Piano Concerto No. 17 in G Major, which does indeed contain several familiar, whistle-like sounds. However, my late colleague at the BBC Natural History Unit, the wonderfully eccentric Jeffery Boswall, always maintained that the composer had purchased his starling several weeks *after* the concerto was first performed in public. So either the bird had learned the melody from hearing it being played, or perhaps Mozart based the theme on a popular tune at the time, which the bird already knew.

Either way, it is clear that he admired the starling itself. After all, starlings are said to make very easy pets, with the added bonus that they are excellent mimics – often of other bird sounds – and can be taught to reproduce human words as well as snatches of music.

In 2017, the Seattle-based writer and naturalist Lyanda Lynn Haupt published *Mozart's Starling*, inspired partly by the composer's story, but also by her own pet starling, Carmen, as Haupt ruefully acknowledged in the book's Prelude:

This book would have taken me half as long to write if it were not for one fact: most of it was composed with a starling perched on my shoulder. Or at least in the vicinity of my shoulder. Sometimes she was standing on top of my head. Sometimes she was nudging the tips of my fingers as they attempted to tap the computer keys. Sometimes she was defoliating the Post-it notes from books where I had carefully placed them to mark passages essential to the chapter I was working on . . . She pooped on my screen. She pooped in my hair.

Haupt explains that she was inspired to write *Mozart's Starling* to discover – from first-hand experience – what Mozart might have learned from such a close relationship with his bird. Having raised starlings while working at an animal rescue centre many years before, Haupt decided to do so again; but this time to write about her experience. As she admitted, things did not exactly go to plan:

> I thought I was bringing a wild starling into my home as a form of research for this book, but this bird had ideas of her own. Instead of settling dutifully into her role as the subject of my grandiose social-scientific-musical experiment, Carmen turned the tables. She became the teacher, the guide, and I became an unwitting student – or, more accurately, a pilgrim, a wondering journeyer who had no idea what was to come.

Like so many people who assume that when it comes to a relationship with nature, they will be the one in charge, she soon learned the truth: that you can take the bird out of the wild, but you cannot take the wild out of the bird.

The starling's extraordinary gifts of mimicry are not confined to music: they can also copy and reproduce human speech, often with uncanny accuracy. Writing in his *Ornithological Dictionary*, first published in 1802, the pioneering ornithologist George Montagu (after whom the elegant raptor Montagu's harrier was named) observed that

> The natural notes of this bird are a shrill whistle and a chattering noise; but in confinement, where it becomes very docile, it is taught to imitate the human voice, and to whistle tunes.

In the *Mabinogion*, a collection of stories in Welsh, collected and compiled from traditional oral tales during the twelfth and thirteenth centuries, the Welsh king's sister Branwen is said to have tamed a starling. She then taught it to speak, before sending it across the Irish Sea with an urgent message for her brothers, asking them to rescue her from captivity.

Branwen
From a water colour by Talbot Hughes, R.O.I.

More than a millennium earlier, in the first century AD, Pliny the Elder wrote of a 'young princess' who kept a starling, which she trained to speak in Greek and Latin – not mere words, but entire sentences – by using morsels of food as a reward. If true, this would put starlings on a par with more celebrated mimics such as parrots. Given that the hill myna – a native of southern Asia – is also an accomplished imitator of human speech, it is likely that the starling's talents have been underrated.

William Shakespeare certainly knew about the bird's unusual talents. In his history play *King Henry IV*, Part 1, the nobleman Hotspur (Sir Harry Percy) declares that because the king has forbidden him to mention his cousin Edmund Mortimer, he will teach a starling to 'speak nothing but Mortimer, and give it him, to keep his anger still in motion'.

More recently, people have taught their pet starlings to say witty or striking phrases, as shown in a widely shared Facebook posting of a bird in the USA, named Jabber, repeating phrases such as 'Gonna give him a kiss', whistling a classical tune and, best of all, doing a note-perfect impersonation of the strange and comical bleeps, clicks and whistles made by the *Star Wars* character R2D2 (which might even have been inspired by the starling).

There are a number of Instagram and TikTok accounts devoted to pet starlings. One of the most popular is 'zephyrthestarling', which features a European starling rescued as a chick in May 2018 after it fell out of its nest in a US parking lot. His owner, self-styled '35-year-old bird mom' Farijuana, began by uploading videos of Zephyr saying 'pretty bird', and whistling the theme to the cult 1960s TV series The Addams Family. But when Zephyr learned to accurately reproduce the theme to the Harry Potter films, the resulting video clip went viral, with more than 30 million views online, and brought his owner close to 150,000 followers on TikTok. Others include Sarah Tidwell, whose Instagram account 'InkyDragon' features 'The Mouth', a nine-year-old R2D2-imitating counterpart.

It is not just musicians and bird-lovers who have kept starlings as pets. The Austrian scientist Konrad Lorenz, who along with Karl von Frisch and Niko Tinbergen was awarded the Nobel Prize for Physiology or Medicine in 1973, found starlings to be ideal animals for detailed study. Being very common, they can easily be taken from the wild soon after fledging, and then hand-reared, while their omnivorous diet, sociable habits and ability to learn make them ideal for keeping in captivity.

Lorenz eventually became very attached to the birds, describing them as 'the poor man's dog', and openly admitting that he loved them. Lloyd and Rose Buck, who keep and train birds to be used in sequences by wildlife filmmakers, consider their starlings to be some of the most affectionate and intelligent of all their birds.

Today, starlings are second only to the domestic pigeon as the species most studied in captivity by scientists. One practical handbook on keeping laboratory animals praises it as 'a model species . . . both inquisitive and a rapid learner', as well as being adaptable enough to be used in a wide range of studies of behaviour, vocalisations and visual perception. The birds' only downside, as the authors note, is the terrible mess they create by defecating everywhere.

One seminal, though controversial, study, published in 2006 in the prestigious journal *Nature*, suggested that starlings could learn to recognise specific patterns of songs. This in turn implied they could learn to understand the patterns of human speech – which might ultimately lead us to understand how our own language evolved in the first place. In the wild, starlings are able not just to learn a whole range of different sounds – known as motifs – but to recognise these when they are sung by other starlings. This enables birds to identify other individuals by listening to their song patterns. By conducting a series of experiments, rewarding the birds when they recognised specific patterns of sound, but withholding food when they did not, the scientists who conducted this 2006 experiment concluded that starlings had highly sophisticated linguistic skills – better, indeed, than another lab animal, the tamarin monkey.

However, other scientists, including the leading US linguistics professor Noam Chomsky, were sceptical, suggesting that what the experiment really showed was the starlings' short-term memory skills rather than their understanding of actual patterns of language. Nevertheless, all agreed that the experiment did show that starlings are both highly intelligent and very rapid learners.

The starling singing in my Somerset garden on New Year's Day was certainly an early bird. But like most resident species, male starlings are usually in full song well before the end of winter, often in February and almost always by the beginning of March. As with all songbirds, this has a dual purpose: to defend a breeding territory against rival males, and to attract a mate.

To maximise his chances of success, a male starling will often combine a series of different song types, typically blending four different song phrases (out of a total vocabulary of as many as thirty-five) into a single series, usually without stopping to take a breath between each.

A groundbreaking 1997 study by the Belgian biologist Professor Marcel Eens of the University of Antwerp found that although we tend to regard the starling's song as a random outpouring of notes, it is actually highly structured and organised, as he discovered when he analysed the sound using spectrograms – visual representations of birdsong:

> A starling song or song bout may last up to one minute and has a complex syntactical and temporal organisation. It is composed of many distinct units that are repeated once, twice or several times before the next unit is introduced . . . Phrases are mostly repeated two or more times before the next 'phrase type' is introduced. A complete starling song bout usually includes four relatively distinct sections or categories of phrases, which tend to occur at particular points.

It's not just about sound, though. While singing, the male will also raise his bill, puff out his throat feathers and spread his wings in a visual courtship display, to enhance his appeal to a prospective mate. This seems to work, as Thomas Bewick observed: 'In pairing time they are extremely frolicsome, flapping, fluttering, and hurrying around and over each other, with odd gestures and tones.'

It is also known that male starlings acquire new versions of their songs, and so revise and renew their aural catalogue from year to year throughout their lifetimes. So although starlings are rarely, if ever, considered to be at the top of the birdsong tree (unlike, for example, the blackbird, song thrush, skylark or nightingale), they are more impressive than they first sound. And just like those more celebrated, varied

and musical songsters, the more varied a male starling's song, the more chance he has of attracting a suitable mate: females are effectively 'programmed' to respond more favourably to a more complex series of notes and phrases.

Like other songbirds, once the pair bond has been formed, the male jealously guards his new mate, following her around to prevent her sneaking off to mate surreptitiously with a rival male.

In the monthly magazine *British Birds* Chris Feare noted that older starlings usually have a more varied and complex repertoire of sounds, and tend to sing for longer periods of time, than their younger counterparts. As a result they often attract mates earlier in the breeding season than their rivals, and have greater reproductive success, raising, on average, more young. This makes sense: to the female, a male that sings a longer and more varied song is probably more experienced and fitter than one with a shorter repertoire and less varied range, and therefore will pass on these genetic advantages to his – and her – offspring. However, there is a downside: when a male bird is singing, he is using energy, and not engaging in what might appear to be more 'useful' behaviours such as feeding or nest-building.

For many years, the fact that male birds that sang louder and longer also appeared to be more successful in both attracting and keeping a mate puzzled scientists, until the Israeli ornithologist Amotz Zahavi came up with a hypothesis called 'the handicap principle'. This suggested that a male bird will signal its high status, and general health and fitness, by indulging in apparently wasteful and unproductive behaviour such as complex song mimicry. This is – forgive the comparison – rather like a man driving a showy and unnecessarily expensive car, or wearing a flashy watch, to show off his supposed 'fitness' to women.

Unusually among British birds, the starling then takes the complexity of his song one stage further, by also being an accomplished mimic. He will often combine snatches of notes or brief phrases from other species of bird – both wild and domestic. Chris Feare and Adrian Craig, authors of the comprehensive monograph *Starlings and Mynas* (1998), noted that 'starlings are not usually thought of as great songsters', at least compared to more conventionally musical singers such as thrushes. But as they pointed out, unlike most other birds, starlings are able to learn new sounds, if and when their environment changes, throughout their entire adult life.

Even after a lifetime's careful observation of the species, Feare is unsure how starlings learn such a wide range of bird calls and songs.

> When I put up a nestbox [for starlings] in my Surrey garden many years ago, the male occupant included excellent curlew calls in its song. There are no curlews for miles around, so where it learned the calls was, and remains, a mystery.

In an article written for the British Library, Jeffery Boswall described the starling as 'the best-known feathered impersonator in Britain and Europe', noting that 'it will pick up sounds from wild birds like buzzards and golden orioles, curlews and tawny owls, and also from domestic hens and geese.' A soundtrack which accompanied Boswall's article, made by the wildlife sound recordist Victor C. Lewis in Herefordshire, included the sounds of jackdaws, house sparrows and even a barking dog! There are also reports of starlings imitating red kites (at their feeding station at Gigrin Farm in mid-Wales), willow warblers and out-of-season common swifts. I have noticed that just outside the Grant Arms Hotel in the Scottish Highlands, a starling regularly imitates the screaming call of the local swifts – sometimes in March or early April, several weeks before these long-distance migrants have arrived back from Africa. Boswall went on to report that in North America, where starlings have been introduced, they will sometimes mimic the complex song of the mockingbird.

Starlings will also incorporate artificial sounds into their vocal repertoire. Boswall noted that one bird in suburban London would regularly cry like a baby, presumably to the consternation of local mothers. In those benighted days when men would regularly utter 'wolf whistles' at any passing woman, starlings learned to do that too.

More seriously, during the final years of the Second World War, starlings in the capital rapidly learned to imitate the terrifying sound of the V-1 flying bombs (the 'V' stood for the German word for 'vengeance') – the 'Doodlebugs' that caused such fear among London's civilian population. I recall my mother telling me that the worst moment was when the V-1s fell silent, which meant the engine had been cut and the bomb was about to land. No doubt many people rushed for cover only to discover – to their relief, though perhaps tinged with annoyance – that the sound was being made by a bird, rather than an actual bomb.

While serving as a captain on the Western Front during the First World War, the Scottish ornithologist and landowner Hugh Gladstone made a number of ornithological observations, which he published in 1919 in his slim volume *Birds and the War*. He described starling flocks that 'would sweep out in a semicircle from some building which had been struck by a shell, and then swing back to it and settle almost before the brick dust had completely cleared away'. Gladstone also reported a similar human response, also as a result of the starling's skills of imitation:

> The powers of mimicry of the starling found scope . . . in the imitation of the three shrill blasts on a whistle used to denote the approach of enemy aeroplanes. 'It was great fun,' he writes, 'to see everyone diving for cover, and I was nearly deceived myself one day.'

On a lighter note, Jeffery Boswall reported that one starling learned to mimic the sound of a football referee's whistle, causing chaos as the players kept stopping play. Starlings are also able to adapt very rapidly to new forms of technology: during the late 1960s they quickly learned to mimic the Trimphone, a handset whose ringtone was a tuneful and rather bird-like warble (oddly reminiscent of the call of the waxwing), rather than the bell-like sound of a traditional telephone.

As domestic technology has continued to develop apace, starlings have always managed to keep up, impersonating the peculiar dial-up tone of early home computer modems, as well as burglar and car alarms and a range of mobile phone ringtones. They are so quick on the uptake that they are sometimes able to learn and reproduce a new sound having only listened to it once or twice.

Like other songbirds, once a pair of starlings has bonded and mated, the male sings less frequently and for a shorter period each day. He will then turn his attention to building a nest: an untidy accumulation of grass, twigs and straw – accurately described by Bewick as 'artless' – which the female lines with feathers, moss and wool to create a suitable place to lay her eggs. Starling nests are usually in holes, ranging from hollows in trees and tree stumps (especially old woodpecker nests) to cracks and crevices in buildings and artificial nestboxes, which are very popular, especially in gardens.

A male starling may go ahead and make a nest even if he hasn't managed to attract a mate, sometimes singing by the entrance and decorating it with flowers or greenery, presumably hoping that this will persuade a passing female to pair up with him. This is not unique among birds – the bowerbirds of New Guinea and Australia create a purpose-built structure to impress their mate – but it is nevertheless unusual to go to such efforts before pairing up with a female.

One study showed that although this habit could have developed because fresh plant material might reduce infestations of parasites, especially when the same nest site is used over several years, this is no

longer the main motive behind the behaviour. Instead it appears to have evolved, like the variety and complexity of the starling's song, because females prefer males with a penchant for home decoration.

The first recorded attempt to encourage starlings to nest – presumably so that they would feed on 'insect pests' – was made by the nineteenth-century explorer and naturalist Charles Waterton (who also brought little owls to his country estate in Yorkshire for exactly the same reason). Described by an eminent American ornithologist as 'a great admirer of the starling', Waterton made cavities in the walls of an old tower, and 'soon every cavity he had made was taken possession of by a pair, and many more would have been thus domiciled had provision been made for them.'

Later, in the German port city of Hamburg, a local horticulturist put up no fewer than 200 wooden nestboxes, each of which was apparently soon occupied. Again, he did so to prevent his precious plants being destroyed by insect pests – and it worked. Given the antipathy shown today by farmers and market gardeners towards starlings on both sides of the Atlantic, this is a salutary warning that these birds may not be quite as harmful as they are portrayed.

In our large and untidy Somerset garden I have from time to time observed nesting starlings. Back in 2010 a pair bred in a hole originally excavated by a great spotted woodpecker on a tall ash tree; later that year they managed to produce a second successful brood. For several months I would watch as the parents came and went, bringing back beakfuls of food for their hungry and demanding chicks.

Although, like most songbirds, starlings are socially monogamous (meaning that they will pair up with a particular female each year to raise a family), some males will hedge their bets by mating with another female and building a second nest, while their original mate is still sitting on her clutch of eggs. However, one Swedish study revealed that the success rate of these second nests was not as high as the first, and that polygamous males, who divide their loyalties between two females, are not usually as successful as those that stick to one mate.

As you might expect from their highly social behaviour in winter, starlings sometimes form small breeding colonies, with more than one nest in the same location. Unusually among songbirds, they also flock together to feed during the breeding season. For that reason, their territories are far smaller than those of other garden birds such as the robin and wren, whose males will fiercely defend not just the immediate space around their nest, but also the wider area in which they feed. In contrast, a typical starling territory extends just a few metres from its nest, just far enough to allow the male to guard the female against any rivals wanting to sneak in and mate with her.

Like many other species that originally nested in natural habitats such as trees, starlings have adapted rapidly to life in cities, where they often find a home in buildings, as the ornithologist Richard Fitter noted in his early account of urban wildlife, *London's Birds* (1949):

> The starling is a well-known hole-nester, and might with some justification be classed among the birds which have transferred from tree-holes to holes in buildings.

Fitter went on to report that a hole beneath a window ledge in Gray's Inn Square, in Central London, was used by successive pairs of starlings for almost three decades during Queen Victoria's reign. It was later celebrated in a verse, 'Starlings', by the early-twentieth-century poet and romantic novelist Mary Webb (whose purple prose was the inspiration for Stella Gibbons' splendid rural satire *Cold Comfort Farm*):

And rusty-feathered fledglings pressed
Close in the nest
Amid the chimney stacks.

In May 1935, celebrations for the Silver Jubilee of King George V meant that London's St James's Park was floodlit each night; this was repeated two years later for the coronation of his son King George VI in May 1937. Fitter reported that fears were raised that the extra light, along with the noise made by the rejoicing crowds, might disturb the nesting starlings. However, a scientist who observed the birds thought it made little or no difference, and that traffic noise was likely to have been a greater problem, as at 4 a.m., when there was very little traffic but the lights were still on, the starlings were apparently silent and asleep.

By the middle of March I am beginning to notice that subtle but inexorable suite of changes that indicate winter is finally reaching its end, and spring is just around the corner. The days lengthen as we head rapidly towards the spring equinox, when day and night will be momentarily equal all around the world.

On the coast, a few miles west of my home, the first wheatears miraculously appear: smart grey and ochre birds, which have flown here all the way from their winter home in sub-Saharan Africa. They bounce up and down on the lichen-covered rocks beside the sea wall, and frequently flash the white rump that gives the species its common name, a corruption of an Anglo-Saxon word which literally means 'white arse'.

In my garden, another new arrival, the chiffchaff, persistently calls out its onomatopoeic name, while flitting about in the blackthorn bushes as these produce their first, snow-white blossom. A week or so later, towards the end of the month, the first blackcap – John Clare's 'March nightingale' – sings its melodic and pleasing song from the elder by my office.

Down on the Avalon Marshes the starlings are still coming in to roost each evening. There are of course far fewer than earlier in the year, but they may still be present in their thousands, although the actual numbers depend on whether the weather has stayed cold or not. Back in late February and early March 2018 the infamous 'beast from the east', as it was dubbed by the tabloids, produced Arctic temperatures and heavy snowfalls across much of Britain, bringing the arrival of spring to a grinding halt. That year, the starling murmurations went on for a couple of weeks longer than usual.

Gradually, though, the numbers do get smaller and smaller, and by the end of March the vast majority of the birds have gone. Most have headed back north and east, to their breeding grounds in Scandinavia and Siberia; only the much smaller breeding population of our local, resident starlings remains. For them, having survived the winter, the next three months are the most crucial in their lives, as they enter the race to reproduce, and pass on their genetic heritage to the next generation.

3

SPRING INTO SUMMER

Of all our native passerine birds, the starling is assuredly one of the most gregarious. Even at the nesting season flocks of unmated starlings are to be seen in the fields, and as soon as the young are grown family parties join forces and may be seen scouring the countryside for food in all manner of places.

David Bannerman, *The Birds of the British Isles* (1953)

The nature poet John Clare would regularly observe starlings nesting in his home village of Helpston, on the edge of the East Anglian fens:

> The starnel builds in chimneys from the view
> And lays an egg like thrushes paley blue . . .

Although starlings' eggs are indeed a pale turquoise blue in colour, they differ from those of the song thrush by being plain, rather than speckled with tiny black spots. They are also slightly more elongated, measuring an average of 30 mm by 21 mm (1.2 by 0.8 in), with a glossy sheen to the surface; while very occasionally they are white, rather than blue, in shade.

Typically, female starlings lay a single egg a day – usually early in the morning – for successive days until the clutch is complete. They generally produce four to six eggs, but sometimes as few as two, or as many as nine. As with other songbirds, delaying the start of incubation until all the eggs have been laid means that the chicks will all hatch out at roughly the same time, between twelve and fifteen days afterwards.

Once the clutch is complete, the female and her mate will take turns to incubate, though she does the lion's share of the duties, sitting on her precious eggs for the whole of each night and most of the day.

From left to right: 1. Willow-warbler, 2. Wood-warbler, 3. Reed-warbler,
4. Marsh-warbler, 5. Sedge-warbler, 6.Grasshopper-warbler, 7. Savi's warbler,
8. Starling, *9. Oriole, 10. Longtailed-tit, 11. Coal-tit, 12. Crested-tit, 13. Marsh-tit,*
14. Great-tit, 15. Blue-tit, 16. Nuthatch, 17. Bearded-reedling, 18. Redbacked-shrike,
19. Woodchat-shrike, 20. Flycatcher, 21. Pied-flycatcher, 22. House-martin,
23. Sand-martin, 24. Swallow.

From time to time the male will temporarily relieve her of her duties, so that she can head away from the nest to feed and regain much-needed energy.

Figures from the long-running Nest Record Scheme by the British Trust for Ornithology (BTO), which has relied on observations provided by amateur observers since it began in 1939, show the median date for first egg-laying is 19 April, although this can range from 6 April to as late as 30 May. Further north in their range, starlings usually begin

nesting much later – those Somerset birds now heading back to Siberia may not lay their eggs until the middle of May.

According to Chris Feare, the semi-colonial nature of starlings means that in any particular area, the laying of these first clutches usually happens within a few days of one another – probably because this reduces the danger of any one nest being predated. And if a clutch is lost, starlings will, like most songbirds, start again with a new set of eggs.

Again like other songbirds, starlings are altricial (also known as nidicolous), rather than precocial (or nidifugous). This means that the chicks are born naked, blind and helpless, and so are entirely dependent on their parents for food and warmth. For the adults this is when the hard work really begins, as they head back and forth to and from the nest during the lengthening hours of daylight to bring back food for their hungry and very demanding chicks.

The results of the adults' efforts are truly incredible. Having tipped the scales at 6 grams at birth, after just twelve days a chick's weight has increased more than twelve-fold, to about 75 grams. That's the equivalent of an average human baby growing from 3.3 kg at birth to almost 40 kg, in less than a fortnight – a weight not normally reached until it is twelve years old! This rapid increase then stabilises, so that when the youngsters fledge, between nineteen and twenty-one days after hatching, they still weigh more or less the same. After they leave the nest, their weight gradually increases, until they reach the typical adult figure of about 85 grams.

Coming across juvenile starlings for the first time often puzzles the unwary observer: the plumage, unlike an adult bird's, is a rather drab, plain brown, and the bill a dark, blackish colour.

In his 1829 work *Journal of a Naturalist*, John Leonard Knapp – described by ornithological biographers Mullens and Swann as 'a disciple of Gilbert White' – wrote a long and detailed account of what he considered to be a separate and distinct species, which he named the 'Brown Starling, or Solitary Thrush (*Turdus solitarius*)'. He described it as 'not an uncommon bird with us', and went on to note that

> it breeds in the holes and hollows of old trees, and, hatching early, forms small flocks in our pastures, which are seen about before the arrival of the winter starling, for which bird, by its manners and habits, it is generally mistaken.

However, after quoting Knapp's account at considerable length, William MacGillivray abruptly debunked it in his characteristically scathing prose, by pointing out that what Knapp considered to be a different species was 'simply a young starling'. To be fair on Knapp, it is an error that has been made ever since.

When it comes to their diet, starlings are often described as 'omnivorous', although as Chris Feare points out, that doesn't actually mean they can eat anything. In practice, they are mainly insectivorous, feeding on a very wide range of insects and other invertebrates. These include flies, spiders, beetles, moths, grasshoppers, crane flies, bees, wasps and ants, as well as larger prey such as snails, earthworms and even on occasion baby lizards and small amphibians. Starlings will also eat seeds, grains, fruits and berries, although they may struggle to digest foods high in sucrose; nor are they able to cope with large quantities of plant material.

In autumn they often feed on fallen and rotting fruit alongside thrushes and blackbirds, and also with butterflies such as red admirals and peacocks. As the fruit rots, the sugars begin to ferment and turn to alcohol, and it has been suggested that if the birds consumed enough of this abundant seasonal bounty they could even get drunk. However, scientific experiments have shown that this is not the case with starlings. It turns out that they are able to use enzymes in their stomach to break down the alcohol much more quickly than we humans can, and therefore avoid the negative consequences of consumption – as well as, presumably, the hangover.

Starlings mostly feed either on or close to the ground, and prefer areas of short grass, such as silage and hay fields, the open areas of parks, and garden lawns, which means that flocks of starlings are a familiar sight in towns and cities as well as in the wider farmed countryside. In rural areas they are often seen in the company of grazing livestock like cattle and sheep. These large animals not only churn up the ground to expose the starlings' prey, but also produce plenty of dung, which also harbours insects and their larvae on which the birds feed. On farmland, feeding starlings are often joined by flocks of other familiar birds, such as rooks and jackdaws.

Although starlings are not always popular amongst farmers, the nature writer and conservationist W. H. Hudson took a different view:

He looks like what he is, a plodding digger in the meadows and pastures . . . There is no doubt that he deserves his reputation as of one of the farmer's feathered helpers . . .

Watching a flock of starlings feed is an object lesson in efficiency. Those birds at the front – where the most food can be found – are constantly displaced by others flying in from the back of the flock, so that they appear to flow across the ground in a dark, constantly moving mass. Then, at some unseen signal, they will all take off and move on to another nearby site, where the whole process begins all over again.

Starlings feed in three basic ways. Most often, as Edmund Selous noted, they do so 'by repeatedly probing and searching the ground with their sharp spear-like bill'. They also feed by hawking for flying insects high in the sky, a behaviour I often see on warm, sunny summer days above my Somerset garden. The third, less frequent and more opportunistic method, is by lunging rapidly forward to grab their victim as it moves across the ground. And of course they will happily take advantage of any food provided by us: from seeds and peanuts in our garden bird feeders to grain and other food given to livestock on farms and in farmyards.

The most common method of feeding is not carried out randomly, as the casual observer might assume. Starlings have developed a novel and striking technique, known as 'open-bill probing', in which the bird pokes its bill into the soil when closed and then, once it is inserted, partially opens it in order to search for prey by sight. As Chris Feare has noted, 'this adaptation also required modified musculature, with stronger muscles to open the bill when it is inserted in the ground. It is a very specialised feeding technique, and few other birds are able to use it.'

Starlings are able to do so because their skull has evolved to be narrower, allowing them to literally peer down their bill and see whether they have found food or not. Other adaptations for ground feeding include stronger legs and feet, and longer toes; hence the jerky, rather comical walk so beloved of the poet Norman MacCaig.

The question as to whether starlings are, on balance, a help or a hindrance to farmers – whether their consumption of harmful insects outweighs their destruction of fruit, seeds and other crops – is tricky and controversial. It has been debated for centuries, with the argument usually being resolved in favour of the farmer rather than the bird.

They have long been regarded as 'pests'. In his 2007 book *Silent Fields: The Long Decline of a Nation's Wildlife*, the conservationist Roger Lovegrove considers a score or more birds that during periods of our history have been on the frontline of what he calls mankind's 'war against nature . . . species which [he] believes conflict with his livelihood'. Not surprisingly, the majority of those birds featured in the book are either raptors (osprey, white-tailed and golden eagles, red kite, hen harrier, buzzard and 'hawks') or corvids (jay, magpie, jackdaw, rook, raven, carrion and hooded crows and even chough). But among those classic 'enemies' are other, more surprising species, including the green woodpecker, kingfisher and the starling.

Lovegrove opens his survey by noting that 'the Starling was not at all a common bird in Britain between the fifteenth and eighteenth centuries', pointing out that, apart from that single reference in *Henry IV*, it is not otherwise mentioned in any of Shakespeare's works. By the 1840s, more than two centuries after the Bard, William MacGillivray was still describing starlings as 'generally distributed but local'.

And yet in the 1566 Vermin Act, passed by Elizabeth I to strengthen a statute introduced by her father Henry VIII three decades earlier, every man, woman and child was urged under the law to kill any wild creature that appeared on the official list of 'vermin', for which they were encouraged by the offer of a financial reward.

For the starling, the bounty was set at one old penny for every dozen birds killed. In today's values that works out at approximately £1.70 per dozen, which doesn't sound very much, but we must remember that a typical unskilled labourer's wage back then was just £5 to £10 a year (roughly £2,000 to 4,000 at today's values), so in real terms this was a much more generous reward than it might first appear.

The original purpose of Henry's 1532 Preservation of Grain Act had been to reduce the numbers of creatures deemed responsible for grain shortages, following a series of bad harvests, and perhaps divert the blame for this onto them rather than government. But given the relative scarcity of the starling at the time, Lovegrove suggests it may have been singled out purely for its predilection for eating soft fruits – especially cherries – just as bullfinches were targeted then, and in some fruit-growing areas still are today. 'A secondary reason [for being on the list of vermin]', he adds, 'may well have been their nuisance value in churches and other buildings', where their collective droppings would be an unwelcome result of their presence.

However, as Lovegrove discovered in his meticulous research, although starlings were included in the act, this apparently did not result in wholesale killings:

> The payment of bounties for starlings is very rare in the hundreds of records that I examined across England and Wales. In fact, only seven instances were found, and almost certainly, with one possible exception, they refer to the removal of Starlings from the parish church.

The only exception was a record from the parish of Monks Kirby, a village between Coventry and Rugby in north-east Warwickshire. There, in one year during the mid-1680s, payments were paid for five shillings, representing approximately 720 (60 dozen) birds, which Lovegrove rightly considered to be 'an impossible number to be found in a church'.

He goes on to discuss the impact of the rise in numbers of starlings in Britain during the course of the nineteenth century, which he (correctly) attributes to improvements in the quality and fertility of the topsoil on lowland farmland. This was as a result of new techniques of deeper ploughing, which would have provided more food for the birds, in the form of soil-dwelling invertebrates such as leatherjackets.

As a result, during the Victorian era starlings cemented their reputation as a 'pest species' for farmers, especially because large flocks would target the germinating seeds of newly planted crops such as wheat, and in autumn and winter concentrate their numbers on livestock farms to feed on fodder provided for cattle.

Those increasingly famous spectacles at winter murmurations did not only attract curious spectators, but also proved a tempting target for local marksmen, as John Leonard Knapp reported in 1829:

The thickness of the flights and the possibility of killing numbers encourages attention. Every village popper notices these flocks and fires into the poor starlings.

Living so closely alongside human beings, starlings were also, unsurprisingly, hunted for food by humans. Indeed, according to Chris Feare, as late as the 1980s – and perhaps beyond – starlings were still being shot at their winter roosts in the UK, for export to continental Europe. He also remembers purchasing a tin of starling pâté at Marseilles Airport, out of simple curiosity, a decision that, having sampled the contents, he soon came to regret: 'I still recall the flavour, for which a taste must only be acquired after many years of subjecting the palate to torture.'

In medieval times starlings, along with thrushes and blackbirds, would certainly have been caught, cooked and eaten, as this account of 'How to take Stares [starlings] with a limed string', in John Ray's 1678 publication *The ornithology of Francis Willughby of Middleton in the county of Warwick* reveals:

> Take a small string of a yard or thereabout long, bind it fast to the Tail of a Stare, having first carefully limed it all over . . . Having found a flock of Starlings, come as near to them as possible, holding your Stare by the wings as near as you can, and let her go to her fellows, which as soon as you shew yourself to them, will presently take wing: Your tail-tied Stare endeavouring to secure herself of her liberty, thrusting herself into the middle of her fellows, will entangle many of them, and so not being able to fly, they will afford a pleasant spectacle in tumbling down to the ground: where you must be ready with a Brush or Besom to strike them down.

In the February 1952 edition of *British Birds* magazine the Scottish ornithologist M.K.M. Meiklejohn reported that in the 1682 version of Giovanni Pietro Olina's *Uccelliera* (first published in 1622) the pioneering Italian naturalist described a simpler and rather ingenious way to trap the birds. This was done by hanging specially made earthenware pots on walls, to encourage starlings to make their nests inside; the young birds would be caught before fledging, then killed and eaten. By the eighteenth century English travellers were still reporting, as the historian Keith Thomas records in *Man and the Natural World* (1983), that when short of food the Italians would eat starlings, and 'other birds which we deem unwholesome'.

In the English countryside starlings and other small birds would have been regularly caught for food at least until the Second World War. My neighbour Rick Popham, whose family have farmed in our Somerset village for at least four generations, remembers his father Reg telling him that on dark winter nights he used to head out on what he called 'bird-batting'. This involved two men walking quietly along the side of thick hedgerows in the fields and lanes around the village, one carrying a net on short poles, the other a gas-fuelled lamp. A third man would walk along the other side of the hedge and beat the bushes with a stick. As the birds flew out they would be momentarily dazzled by the lamp and caught in the net.

These birds – which would almost certainly have included starlings, as well as members of the thrush family such as blackbirds, redwings and fieldfares – would then be taken home, plucked, cooked and eaten, a much-needed source of protein at a time of wartime food shortages and rationing. During the Second World War, it was even reported that starlings were being sold for food in the exclusive London department store, Harrods.

As well as the occasional threat from human gastronomes, starlings, like all small and medium-sized songbirds, also face constant danger from both avian and mammalian predators. Not surprisingly, given how common and ubiquitous starlings are, they are hunted by almost all birds of prey, including harriers, buzzards, kites, sparrowhawk and goshawk, our four falcon species (kestrel, hobby, merlin and peregrine), all five breeding owls (tawny, barn, little, long-eared and short-eared), and opportunist feeders such as carrion crows. Various mammals, including wild predators such as stoat and weasel, along with domestic dogs and cats, also occasionally catch and kill starlings.

None of these have a major effect on starling populations, for the simple reason that the numbers taken from any one flock or roost will never be very high.

However, circumstances do sometimes change the behaviour of predators, and place starlings under greater threat than before. During the Covid-19 lockdowns from March 2020 onwards, the number of feral pigeons in London fell dramatically, as a result of a major reduction in the birds' food normally provided by humans. Consequently the capital's peregrines – a population now at an all-time high of roughly thirty pairs – who had been dining predominantly on pigeon, were forced to turn to other common and more available species. As well as London's famous rose-ringed parakeets, the peregrines' main victims were starlings, which were killed in far greater numbers than before.

Presumably when the lockdowns ended and life returned to normal, the falcons reverted to hunting the plumper and more satisfying pigeons. As the RSPB's Richard Gregory says, this 'illustrates that the fabric of life around us is delicately balanced, and even small changes can have profound cascading effects on nature.'

If I were to compile a 'league table' of birds featured in literature and culture – especially poetry – the skylark and nightingale would be well out in front. They have been celebrated from Greek and Roman times to the present day, most famously in John Keats's poem 'Ode to a Nightingale' and his contemporary Percy Bysshe Shelley's 'To a Skylark'. Hot on their heels would be other much-loved and familiar birds: the brief and anonymous thirteenth-century poem 'Sumer is icumen in', celebrating the spring arrival of the cuckoo, Gerard Manley Hopkins' dazzling 'As Kingfishers Catch Fire', Edward Lear's humorous 'Owl and the Pussycat', Thomas Hardy's thoughtful and atmospheric 'The Darkling Thrush' and Edgar Allan Poe's Gothic-horror tale, 'The Raven'.

The same is true of birds in classical music, where not surprisingly the most tuneful songsters are the ones most often used as inspiration: notably in Beethoven's Symphony No. 6 (the Pastoral), which features the nightingale (flute), quail (oboe) and cuckoo (two clarinets), as well as in many works by the twentieth-century French composer (and serious amateur ornithologist) Olivier Messiaen.

A few examples aside – including the enchanting story of Mozart and his pet starling already told in chapter 2 – we have to search quite hard to find examples of writers and composers being inspired by the common-or-garden starling. When it does appear – in both poetry and prose – it tends to be as a brief mention of a murmurating winter flock or, as in John's Clare's poem, part of a wider description of a rustic scene rather than the subject. It's almost as if starlings are regarded as simply part of our rural landscape: the supporting cast, lurking in the background, rather than those other, more showy lead actors like the skylark and the nightingale.

As if to confirm this, one recent anthology, *The Poetry of Birds* (2009), compiled by Tim Dee and Simon Armitage, includes seven poems each for the skylark, nightingale and swallow, and five for another familiar bird, the house sparrow. The starling gets just three. These are by Ted Hughes ('Starlings Have Come', focusing on the winter murmurations), David Hartnett ('Mimics', on the birds' gift for imitation) and

W. N. Herbert ('The Flock in the Firth', an extraordinary verse written in Scots dialect, about witnessing a gathering of starlings as the poet crosses the Forth Rail Bridge).

A notable exception is the frequent appearance of starlings as the subject of haiku poems, those brief, intense representations of moments in time. *Wing Beats: British Birds in Haiku*, a delightful anthology compiled by John Barlow and Matthew Paul published in 2008, includes more than a dozen examples, including the one quoted in this book's Prologue. Aptly for the starling, these are often rooted in familiar domesticity, such as this striking example from Barlow himself:

> steam rises
> over the workmen's kettle
> starling whistles

Other haikus in *Wing Beats* feature starlings on TV aerials, pecking at ice on a birdbath or drinking from cracks in the pavement. Likewise, Rob Cowen's lovely poem which I have used as this book's epigraph is also based on the birds' easy familiarity and constant presence in our lives. It is rather apt that these town-dwelling poets celebrate a bird that lives right alongside us, yet whose presence we often overlook.

Starlings may not be as popular with poets as larks and nightingales, yet they appear in literature and culture a very long way back. In the ancient world starlings were often associated with the Roman goddess Venus (equivalent to the Greek Aphrodite), while the starling's ability to mimic other birds, along with human and artificial sounds, was also recognised by the Ancient Romans. This was mentioned by

Pliny in the first century AD, who also reported that, as a young man, the Emperor Nero kept a pet starling, which he taught to speak Greek and Latin.

Much earlier, around the sixth century BC, the Greek storyteller Aesop told the tale of a farmer whose wheat was constantly being stolen by marauding starlings and rooks. When he and his boy tried to hit the birds with a slingshot, the clever starlings warned the rooks and they escaped. Eventually he played a trick on the birds and managed to kill them.

Starlings also figure widely in popular folklore. Across much of Europe, as one of the first species to start nesting in late winter, they are welcomed as a sign of the coming of spring, especially because they often nest close to people's homes, so their nest-building is perhaps more visible than other, more secretive birds'.

Flocks of starlings are also supposed to foretell cold or wet weather, though given that they appear in large numbers in late autumn and winter this is hardly surprising. In *Weather Lore*, a popular collection of 'sayings, proverbs and rules concerning the weather' (first published in 1898, and often reprinted since), the folklorist Richard Inwards observes that 'If starlings and crows congregate together in large numbers, expect rain.'

According to *Bird Facts and Fallacies*, published in the late 1920s by another collector of folklore, Lewis R. W. Loyd, in Brittany it is said that large gatherings of starlings signify impending cold weather. 'On 2 December 1925,' Loyd adds, writing about a very cold spell with severe frosts,

> many thousands settled in the evening on St Paul's Cathedral, and their appearance in this case entirely supported the Breton belief.

In other cultures around the world, starlings have various symbolic meanings. In China they are said to bring good fortune and prosperity, and in Japan the white-cheeked (or grey) starling (*mukudori*) represents eternal love. However, this species' recent habit of roosting in cities appears to have somewhat dented that romantic reputation.

4

SUMMER INTO AUTUMN

They frequently rose into the air ... turning and
twisting about like flycatchers, though with less
graceful movements.

Edmund Selous, *Bird Watching* (1901)

One hot summer's day a few years ago I was relaxing in a hammock in our Somerset garden, drifting in and out of a light afternoon doze, when something must have stirred me – perhaps the chipping call of a great spotted woodpecker, or the gentle twittering of swallows in the clear blue sky.

Whatever it was, I opened my eyes and noticed a loose flock of birds gliding high above. At first I assumed these were swallows, which regularly hawk with their youngsters for flying insects at this time of year. Something wasn't quite right, though. I took a closer look, and realised they were starlings – dozens of them – flitting around in the warm and rising air, from time to time closing their wings to brake before grabbing an unseen flying insect with their beaks.

I soon realised I was witnessing what has come to be known as 'flying ant day'. This event, which I vaguely recall from my childhood, occurs every year at the height of summer, usually soon after a period of heavy rainfall, when the weather conditions are suitably hot and humid. Swarms of our most abundant species, the black garden ant *Lasius niger*, are triggered by these warm temperatures, which encourage the young queen ants to leave the safety of their nest and mate with male flying ants – humorously dubbed by one scientist as being 'pretty much just flying sperm'.

After their aerial mating, each queen will drop back down to earth, shed her wings and make a new nest in the soil. She will never need to fly or mate again, as she has enough sperm stored away from that one series of sexual encounters. Following their brief moment of glory the males, their reproductive duties now over, simply die.

Meanwhile, the starlings have a new and plentiful, albeit temporary, food source to exploit – which they do. As Chris Feare explains, although starlings' long and pointed wings are designed for speed rather than manoeuvrability, meaning they are far less adept at aerial hunting than swallows, martins and swifts, they nevertheless will indulge in flycatching when the rewards for doing so are so bountiful.

By now, with the breeding season mostly over, starlings are beginning to form flocks: small at first, but gradually reaching groups of a hundred birds or more. Although these are far less large and impressive than the huge groupings we see in late autumn and winter, they nevertheless become more and more noticeable with each passing week. These flocks are made up of both the dark adults and the paler, milk-chocolate-brown juveniles, who no doubt have learned that their parents – and other mature birds – know how and where to find food, so stick close by.

Summer is a time of abundance, and therefore the period when the adults moult into a fresh new plumage for the colder weather to come, usually starting the process a few weeks earlier than the youngsters. As with most songbirds, the moult occurs in a specific and set order: starting with the wings, and the shedding of the innermost primary feathers (the longest wing feathers), followed methodically by the next primary, and so on, until all ten have been replaced. The new feathers take between three and four weeks to grow to full length, with the entire process taking just over three months. Other feather areas to be replaced include the secondaries and tertials on the wing, and the twelve tail feathers, a process usually starting in August. At the same time as the wing feathers are being replaced, the bird sheds and replaces its body feathers.

This results in an easily observed change in the bird's appearance, from the glossy, dark breeding plumage to the spottier and more matt non-breeding garb, which will remain until the following spring, the paler feather tips gradually wearing away until the bird appears glossy again. By moulting over a relatively long period, in sequence, starlings never lose their ability to fly – unlike ducks, which become flightless for a brief period in late summer and early autumn.

Like other birds, once they have moulted – and indeed during the rest of the year – starlings need to ensure they keep their plumage as clean and neat as possible. Matted or dirty feathers make the bird more vulnerable not just to predators, but also to diseases. Starlings are especially prone to various body and plumage parasites, including ticks and mites, which also infest their nests.

In one study of 300 starlings, carried out in six US states in the early 1950s, every single bird harboured at least one parasite: 95 per cent had internal parasites (mostly worms), while virtually all carried external parasites – mites, ticks or fleas – on their feathers.

To try to counter these infestations, and keep their plumage clean and in good condition, starlings are regular visitors to garden bird baths and ponds. On a warm summer or early autumn day they sometimes arrive in twos and threes, but often in large flocks, each bird jostling with its fellow bathers and covering its feathers with water, to get as clean as they can in a brief but hopefully productive visit. They will also take advantage of the water to drink, by dipping their bills and then lifting up their heads so that the precious liquid flows down their throat – for, like other songbirds, they are unable to swallow.

A more unusual way of keeping clean is by 'anting', a process by which the birds find an active colony of ants, then pick up several at a time with their bill and use them to 'wipe' their plumage. This provokes the unfortunate ants to discharge formic acid, which might serve to repel any ectoparasites. Oddly, however, researchers have shown that anting appears to have no effect at all on the presence or absence of parasites. Indeed, some scientists have suggested that the reason birds use ants is simply because they like the sensory feelings the behaviour gives rise to, while others have compared this rather bizarre behaviour to human spa treatments, or even glue-sniffing!

Other ways starlings preen include the more conventional methods of using their bills to clean their feathers, or their feet to scratch. Some social species of starling engage in 'allopreening', in which the two members of a pair mutually preen one another – a romantic as well as a practical solution to the problem of keeping clean and tidy. Unlike sparrows, however, starlings have not been observed 'dust-bathing': wallowing in fine dust and dirt to remove the oily secretions from their feathers.

After a strange summer's weather, with high temperatures in June followed by a rather cooler and unsettled July and August, September opened with a record heatwave – a week of temperatures in the low 30s, contradicting the Met Office's strange insistence that autumn starts at the beginning of that month (whereas of course it actually begins later in September, at the time of the autumn equinox).

By early afternoon it had become far too warm for me to work comfortably in my garden office, so I used this excuse to head down to my local patch on the Somerset coast. Here, by the Rivers Huntspill, Parrett and Brue, a light breeze made things a touch more bearable. In the copse just north of Huntspill Sluice I came across a classic sight of late summer: a flock of fifty or so juvenile starlings, chuntering softly to one another as they perched on the bare upper twigs of a tree.

I say juvenile, but these were more like a crowd of unruly teenagers, poised halfway between childhood and adulthood. For although they had the youngsters' plain, pale buffish-brown headgear, the back, belly and tail were much darker, and covered with the spots and speckles of adult plumage, reminding me of children who have dressed up in their parents' clothes, yet still retain an innocent, open countenance.

As if in response to an unseen signal, the birds suddenly dropped off their perches and flew the short distance to the grassy area by the river Parrett. Because this area is covered twice daily by the ebb and flow of the tide, it is an ideal place to probe the damp soil for invertebrates.

They didn't have it all to themselves. Small flocks of pied wagtails, along with a few yellow wagtails, accompanied by a perky wheatear, bulky skylarks and more slender meadow pipits, were also taking advantage of this temporary habitat to feed for a few hours before the waters rose again. But there was plenty of room for them all, and the starlings continued to forage happily, their newly acquired glossy plumage occasionally glinting in the afternoon sun.

Nearer my home, the telephone lines alongside a farm were laden with more post-breeding birds, which would have nested in the barns nearby, along with another species that does so, the swallows. I stopped my bicycle for a closer look, as first the starlings, then the swallows, dropped off the lines at some unseen signal: the starlings usually landing on the ground to forage for food, the swallows swooping up into the air to snatch flying insects.

In a month or so those starlings would begin to head down to the Avalon Marshes, to join birds from far farther afield for those nightly murmurations. By then the swallows would be long gone, having crossed continental Europe, the Mediterranean Sea, the Sahara Desert and equatorial Africa, to roost in South African reedbeds more than 10,000 kilometres from home. How different the lives of neighbouring birds can be.

Meanwhile, other starlings, along with many other species of birds, are travelling south and west, from northern Europe and Russia, to spend the autumn and winter here before returning north and east to breed. Britain and Ireland – 'the British Isles', to use a convenient if politically dubious term – are home to at least as many winter visitors, in terms of individuals, if not species, as summer ones.

The two dominant groups are wildfowl – ducks, geese and swans, which arrive from Arctic Canada, Greenland, Iceland, Scandinavia and Siberia – and waders, which also hail from a wide swathe of the northern hemisphere. They choose to come here for one simple reason: our relatively mild winter climate. A relative lack of snow and ice, and generally above-average temperatures, means reliable and accessible supplies of food, especially on our coastal marshes and estuaries, as well as lakes, reservoirs and gravel pits further inland.

With such huge numbers of large, colourful and showy birds on display, it would be understandable to ignore the smaller migrants that also spend the autumn and winter months here: most notably, redwings, fieldfares and starlings. In the case of starlings, they are especially easy to overlook, given that, unlike the two 'winter thrushes', the bird is such a common and widespread breeding species in Britain.

In 1967, according to the BTO's *Winter Atlas* (published in 1986), the number of starlings wintering here was estimated at 37 million, which dwarfs the first *Breeding Atlas* estimate of between 4 and 7 million breeding pairs. In the half century since then, however, the number of both breeding and wintering starlings has fallen dramatically. The latest BTO survey, from 2016, estimates roughly 1.8 million breeding pairs: a fall of between over half and three-quarters. We don't have an updated estimate for wintering birds but, given the disappearance of so many once-famous murmurations, and the reduction in numbers at those that remain, I would be surprised if more than 10 million starlings now overwinter here – again, a fall of around three-quarters in fifty years.

However, despite the definite decline – and disappearance – of many urban roosts, Chris Feare believes there may still be more elsewhere than we suppose:

> I have been surprised at the number of murmurations being reported on Facebook sites. Former city centre roosts have disappeared, but the number and size of rural roosts has really surprised me!

Estimates of the numbers of birds at these autumn and winter gatherings are always just that – estimates. But thanks to the hard work of amateur and professional ornithologists, who carry out regular surveys of birds throughout the year, we can track the comparative rises and falls in bird populations.

One way is through bird ringing: placing a small, light and unobtrusive metal band, containing a unique serial number, on birds caught in a mist-net, or ringed as juveniles in the nest. Having been weighed, measured and ringed, each bird is released back into the wild, with the hope that, at some point in the future, it will be trapped again or found dead, so its movements can be traced. Coincidentally, the very first bird ever to be fitted with a ring of this kind was a starling.

On 6 June 1890, a Danish schoolmaster and amateur ornithologist named Hans Christian Cornelius Mortensen trapped two starlings in one of his nestboxes. He placed a narrow ring, which he had made from zinc, onto each bird's leg, each marked with a simple pair of inscriptions, one written in ink, the other engraved directly onto the metal.

Almost immediately Mortensen was dissatisfied with his work, mainly because the rings were too heavy, and so impeded the bird's natural movement and behaviour. Despite this initial setback he continued to refine his idea, and nine years later, on 5 June 1899, he attached a newly designed, home-made (and much lighter) aluminium ring onto the leg of a starling. It was marked with the inscription 'VIBORG 1', after Viborg, the city in central Jutland where he lived. By the end of that year he had ringed no fewer than 165 starlings, which he caught using an ingenious automatic closing mechanism on his nestboxes.

Over the next few years Mortensen went on to ring more than 1,500 birds from a wide range of species, including gulls, ducks, herons and white storks, as well as starlings. He was helped by a grant from the Carlsberg Foundation (run by the lager company), which augmented his meagre salary as a schoolteacher. He also took his students out into the field to observe birds and other wildlife for themselves; again, he was one of the very first people to do so.

Hans Christian Mortensen died on 7 June 1921, aged sixty-four. Other, better-known names, such as Harry Witherby and Sir Arthur Landsborough Thomson in Britain, and John James Audubon and Ernest Thompson Seton in North America, often get the credit for launching the practice of bird ringing – one that has taught us so much about the lives and movements of birds. But this humble Dane was the man who really started it off. And the bird he chose for his pioneering experiments was the starling.

Another great pioneer of migration studies was William Eagle Clarke. Born in Leeds in 1853, he originally trained as a surveyor and civil engineer, but eventually turned his passion for birds into his life's work as a professional ornithologist – one of very few people to do so at that time. He became the curator of the Leeds Museum in his early thirties, and a few years later, in 1888, moved north to join the department of natural history at the Royal Scottish Museum in Edinburgh (now the National Museum of Scotland), where he worked until his retirement in 1921.

Eagle Clarke studied migratory birds at various locations around continental Europe, but his greatest insights came when he teamed up with another pioneer ornithologist, Mary Russell, Duchess of Bedford, on the small island of Fair Isle, between Orkney and Shetland in the North Sea.

Today Fair Isle is arguably the best-known birding location in Britain – and one of the most celebrated in the world – for its seemingly magnetic ability to attract avian wanderers from all corners of the northern hemisphere. To date this small speck of land, with an area of less than 8 square kilometres (roughly 3 square miles) has recorded almost 400 different species of bird, including no fewer than twenty-seven sought-after 'firsts for Britain' – birds hitherto unseen in the British Isles.

Between 1909 and 1914, the Duchess of Bedford and William Eagle Clarke visited the island many times, with their observations featuring in his two-volume *Studies in Bird Migration*, published in 1912. But the author wasn't only interested in rare vagrants: he also included a detailed chapter on 'The Migration of the Starling'.

He opened his account with a paradoxical warning about the difficulties of studying the complex and unpredictable movements of such a common and widespread bird:

> The migrations of the starling observed in Great Britain and Ireland are of a singularly varied nature, being performed with great frequency and at all seasons. These . . . are due to a number of causes – among others, to its gregarious and capricious nature, the varying degree of its migratory instincts . . . its dependence upon supplies of food which change not only with the season but from year to year . . . peculiarities which result in innumerable movements, many of them of a partial or wholly irregular nature.

He also noted some aspects of the starling's life which might surprise us. For example, in parts of south-west England (notably Devon and Cornwall), the species was then still mainly a winter visitor, having only recently begun breeding there. Just over half a century later, by the time of the first BTO *Atlas* in the late 1960s and early 1970s, the starling had become a common resident breeder in the South-west.

Eagle Clarke separated the starling's migrations and movements into different stages. These began with local movements in the early summer – 'as soon as the young . . . are able to shift for themselves' – to be succeeded soon afterwards by what he called 'emigrations', as some of our breeding birds headed away from our shores, in late July, August and early September, to spend the autumn and winter in south-west Europe. 'These movements of departure are performed during the night,' he recorded,

> or the earliest hours of the morning, and hence for the most part escape notice, but I have received during the past few years much valuable information regarding them from the Eddystone lighthouse [off the south coast of Cornwall], the situation of which is singularly favourable for the making of such observations.

Not so favourable for the birds themselves, however: he went on to describe a major movement of starlings past Eddystone one night in autumn 1901, when sixty-seven birds were found dead beneath the lighthouse. They had been dazzled by its lantern, while hundreds more would have fallen into the surrounding sea and drowned.

From the last week of September, just after those British breeding birds have finally left, the first immigrants from continental Europe appear, and continue to arrive throughout October and into early November. This is followed, soon afterwards, by birds arriving from further afield, including Scandinavia and Siberia. It is these which form the majority of the birds we see at our winter roosts.

Not all of them stay in Britain for the winter, however, as Eagle Clarke reported:

> At the end of October 1870 a large flock was encountered 300 miles west of Scilly, and on 23 October 1876 one alighted on HMS *Alert* between capes Farewell and Clear [the southernmost points, respectively, of Greenland and Ireland], when 517 miles from the latter.

It is interesting, though perhaps fruitless, to speculate whether some of these westward-heading birds might have made it all the way across the Atlantic, to make landfall in Newfoundland, the nearest land to where that hitchhiking individual was observed. Of course, that would only be known if starlings had not been introduced into North America in the late nineteenth century, thus masking the arrival of any genuine vagrants since then.

Since Eagle Clarke's day there have been considerable advances in our knowledge of how, when and why birds migrate, thanks not least to developments in technology such as tracking devices which, when attached to a bird, provide vital information about the timing and geography of its travels.

At the turn of the millennium, however, we were still relying mostly on a combination of ringing recoveries and field observations to discover the routes of migratory birds. Published in 2002 but based on recoveries of ringed birds started almost a century ago, in 1909, *The Migration Atlas: Movements of the Birds of Britain and Ireland* provided detailed analysis of millions of records. In the case of the starling these included over 1.2 million ringed birds, which yielded over 40,000 recoveries (including 4,000 birds originally ringed abroad and later recovered in Britain).

Most were ringed at those huge winter roosts, which provide the ideal opportunity to catch large numbers of birds at once, but some were ringed as chicks in the nest. As to the circumstances in which the birds were recovered (the vast majority, over 96 per cent, being found dead), the greatest number (35 per cent) were killed by domestic predators – mostly cats. Almost all the rest were the result of 'human activities', presumably including birds killed by motor vehicles, though the small number of foreign recoveries, all from continental Europe, were mostly shot or trapped.

The findings confirmed that there are two substantial populations of starlings in Britain and Ireland: the breeding birds, which are virtually all resident, and a substantial number of migratory birds arriving from the north and east during the autumn, and staying here for the winter. Chris Feare, who wrote the *Atlas* account, explains:

> In late October and early November large numbers of Starlings . . . can be seen arriving on the Lincolnshire coast in flocks. Arrival begins soon after dawn and lasts until early afternoon, indicating that most of the migration is diurnal. Most flocks do not stop on the coast but continue inland.

The Migration Atlas also showed the geographical origin of starlings arriving here, which largely came from an east-north-east direction, but ranged as far as Norway in the north to the Netherlands, northern Germany and northern Poland – and almost as far east as the Russian Urals, a journey of over 3,000 km (almost 2,000 miles).

The birds stay here for between four and five months, usually leaving straight from their roosts early in the morning, in March or April, to head back to their breeding grounds.

5

AUTUMN INTO WINTER

An immense flock of starnels settled on an ash tree in
the orchard & when they took wing it was like a large
roll of thunder.

John Clare, *Natural History Diary* (4 November 1841)

Just before dusk one day in late autumn 2006, a few months after I had moved from London to Somerset with my young family, I went out of our back door. Our home – a farmhouse dating back to the early nineteenth century – stands directly opposite another, smaller and even older cottage, with a narrow driveway in between. As I stepped outside I heard a strange, whooshing sound, which made me look up. Within a heartbeat its origin became clear, as a tight flock of two or three thousand birds appeared from a northerly direction over the cottage, and then moments later disappeared southwards, behind our house.

They were, of course, starlings, racing as fast as they could towards the Avalon Marshes, and their evening roost. I was left with the hazy imprint of these small, dark birds on my retina, and that extraordinary whooshing sound echoing in my ears.

This was not the first time I had encountered flocks of starlings in my garden. My diary notes that, in late August of my first year there,

starling numbers began to increase: sometimes large flocks overhead or on the bramble bushes; and also about sixty on the cottage roof one morning, where they annoyed the resident male house sparrow!

In early autumn, then, and every year afterwards, they have come to feed on our elderberries where, as the larger and dominant species, they soon see off the smaller chiffchaffs, blackcaps and occasional lesser whitethroat. Starlings also feed in the apple orchard next door, or on the lush autumnal harvest of deep crimson hawthorn berries, which line the narrow country lanes behind our house. This bounty is also enjoyed by visiting redwings and fieldfares, which rise up into the air on the fresh autumn winds as I pass. The starlings occasionally come to bathe in our garden pond, splashing about like a group of rowdy kids at a paddling pool.

On warm afternoons in October – which seem to be getting more frequent nowadays, as a result of climate change – I sometimes see flocks of starlings hawking for insects overhead, as they usually do on hot, sunny days in late summer. And on colder mornings from November onwards, if I head out into the garden just before sunrise, I see a steady flow of starlings heading purposefully north-west, like RAF squadrons, off to feed for the day in the local fields, or farther afield on the saltmarshes and mudflats along the Somerset coast.

By the end of October, the starling flocks are already starting to gather each evening on the Avalon Marshes, although in far smaller numbers than later in the season – the thousands, rather than the tens or hundreds of thousands. These seasonal gatherings have long been known to naturalists, the early nineteenth-century ornithologist Thomas Bewick, based in Northumberland, writing that

In the autumn they fly in vast flocks, and may be known at a great distance, by their whirling mode of flight, which Buffon [a distinguished French ornithologist] compares to a sort of vortex, in which the collective body performs a uniform circular revolution, and at the same time continues to make a progressive advance.

Bewick's contemporary George Montagu quoted detailed observations from another Northumberland naturalist and artist, Prideaux John Selby.

> In the autumnal and hyemal [winter] months these birds gather in immense flocks . . . Before they retire to rest, they produce various manoeuvres in the air, the whole frequently describing rapid revolutions round a common centre. This peculiar flight will sometimes continue for nearly half an hour, before they become finally settled for the night.

But Bewick and Selby were far from the first people to observe these nightly gatherings. Almost two millennia earlier, the Roman historian Pliny was perceptively noting that 'It is peculiar to starlings . . . to fly in crowds, and wheel about as it were in a ball, all tending to the middle of the band.'

Other observers have noticed that roosting starlings often show a preference for reed beds, which, being surrounded by water, are likely to provide added protection against land-based predators such as foxes and badgers. Another observer from the same period as Bewick and Montagu, the Revd William Barker Daniel, noted in his 1801 book *Rural Sports* that one area of reeds, being grown to produce thatch for the roofs of houses, suffered damage 'to the tune of one hundred pounds in one night [equivalent to almost £10,000 at today's values!]'. He went on to explain, rather graphically, that 'it was not only that the starlings bent the stems . . . but by their abundant excrement the reeds became soiled, and consequently less saleable.'

Edward Grey, Viscount of Fallodon (near the coast just north of Alnwick, in Northumberland), was not only Britain's longest-serving Foreign Secretary to date (serving for eleven years from 1905 to 1916),

but also a distinguished amateur ornithologist. In *The Charm of Birds* (1927), a bestselling book written towards the end of his lifetime, Grey described the flight of a pre-roosting gathering of starlings – what he called 'a vast globe' – over his country estate:

> They fly close together, and there are many evolutions and swift turns, yet there is no collision: the impulse to each quick movement or change of direction seems to seize every bird simultaneously.

It appeared, he went on to speculate, that the flock had become a single organism, rather than a collection of individuals:

> It is as if for the time being each bird had ceased to be a separate entity and had become a part of one sentient whole: one great body, the movement of whose parts was co-ordinated by one impulse or one affecting them all at the same moment.

Huge flocks of starlings have always roosted in dense forestry plantations. In his *History of British Birds*, published in the mid-nineteenth century, William Yarrell reported that the Dean of Wells, Dr Edmund Goodenough, had discovered a large roost on an estate at King's

Weston (on the western edge of Bristol between the rivers Avon and Severn), owned by a W. Miles Esq.

> This locality is an evergreen plantation . . . to which the birds repair in an evening – I was going to say, and I believe I might in truth say – by millions, from the low grounds about the Severn . . . By packing in such myriads upon the evergreens, they have stripped them of their leaves . . . and have driven the pheasants, for which this plantation was intended, quite away from the ground. In the daytime, when the birds are not there, the stench is still excessive. Mr Miles was about to cut the whole plantation down to get rid of them . . . but I begged him not to on account of the curiosity of the scene, and he has since been well pleased that he abstained.

Today we tend to think of starlings roosting mostly in reed beds or, if we have longer memories, on city buildings. But there are still some that roost in forestry plantations, as was recently shown in the woodland episode of the landmark BBC TV series *Wild Isles*. Sir David Attenborough's commentary sets the scene:

> This plantation, hemmed in by farmland on one side, and Bodmin Moor on the other, is cold, dark and inhospitable. But birds are using this wood as a temporary home, and its branches are caked with the evidence. As the late winter sun begins to sink, the tenants return.

Those tenants are, of course, starlings: up to a million of them, flying in from the surrounding fields and moors. Using the latest drone technology, producer Chris Howard and wildlife cameraman Steven McGee-Callender give us a unique aerial perspective as the flocks arrive. Then they inject the drama: a buzzard soaring overhead, 'hoping to snatch a weak bird from amongst the flock', followed by a peregrine, whose brooding manifestation forces the flock to 'swirl and coalesce as they react to the predator's presence'.

As the light fades, the starlings drop down into the forest canopy, where the remote camera expert Jo Charlesworth has carefully rigged several cameras to film the birds as they settle, and where they – and we – assume they are now safe. But in one of the most dramatic British wildlife sequences ever shot, the veteran cameraman Mark Yates uses a thermal camera to reveal the presence of a nocturnal predator. We watch as a barn owl hovers just above the roost, causing the starlings perched beneath to panic, before it drops down and snatches a single, unfortunate bird from the flock.

In the popular ten-minute slot at the end of the programme, Chris Howard reveals just how disagreeable it was to film that revolutionary new sequence, because of the thick and glutinous layer of starling droppings covering the forest floor:

> It was one of the most unpleasant places I've ever had to work – it really did stink, and the droppings were all over our clothes, in our hair, they got everywhere!

But even worse was to come: 'Just as it was all coming together the birds disappeared – we somehow lost a million starlings!'

The birds had flown to another, inaccessible wood, about 20 miles away, and soon afterwards they headed off to their breeding grounds. At this point the team only had two or three shots with the thermal camera – nowhere near enough for a full sequence. They had to wait almost a full year for the starlings to return, which fortunately they did. This allowed the filmmakers to use the thermal camera to capture that memorable sequence, for us to enjoy in the comfort of our own homes – without having to endure that terrible smell.

The question I am most often asked about the starling murmurations is a deceptively simple one, with a rather more complicated answer: exactly *why* do they gather in such numbers in the first place?

Of course, many other species of birds come together to roost. I've watched several hundred pied wagtails on a winter's evening in Newton Abbot, in south Devon, all packing together into the branches of a single, well-lit tree in the middle of the town's pedestrian precinct. Then there is the huge winter gathering, of an estimated 50,000 to 80,000 rooks and jackdaws, which heads every evening towards Buckenham Marshes in east Norfolk, a phenomenon celebrated by Mark Cocker in his 2008 book *Crow Country*.

Impressive though these numbers are, though, they are dwarfed by the figures in starling roosts. The Avalon Marshes murmuration regularly tops 250,000 birds, on occasions reaching half a million or more, while more than a million birds have been counted at RSPB Otmoor in Oxfordshire, and a roost in the city of Rome is thought to reach 3 million on some occasions.

Yet even this pales in comparison with what some old-timers tell me: that a couple of decades ago, as many as *seven million* starlings would come together on these cold winter evenings. The lower numbers today reflect the decline in the starling population both here and abroad – the majority of the birds at these winter roosts have travelled here from continental Europe; many from as far afield as Russia.

As to why they gather in such vast numbers, there are two favourite – and both plausible – suggestions. The first is that by joining forces in such large numbers the birds can protect themselves from predators; the second is that they are better able to keep warm when huddling up with one another in the roost.

Let's start with the anti-predation theory. Fundamentally, this comes down to numbers and the law of chance: the more birds each individual stays with, the less likely they are to be picked off by a passing hawk or falcon. Scientists call this the 'dilution effect' – as the numbers increase, so the chances of any one bird being attacked and killed reduce dramatically. This rule doesn't just apply to starlings – or, indeed, just to birds. Any living creatures that gather together – from herds of antelopes on the African savannah to shoals of fish in the sea, as well as swarms of insects and other invertebrates – find safety in numbers.

There is another factor at play, which also applies to smaller groups such as garden birds on feeders, or breeding colonies of seabirds – indeed, to almost any large gathering of birds, at any time of year. Put simply, the more individuals there are in a flock, the higher the likelihood that at least one of them will spot any incoming danger, and sooner than a smaller number of birds would.

It's also important to understand how a predator like a peregrine or sparrowhawk hunts its prey. You might imagine that the easiest way for them to catch a starling would be to simply dive into the flock at random and grab whatever they hit. In fact, the opposite is the case: a predator will get visual 'focus-lock' on a specific individual – possibly a bird that is slightly isolated in the group or just one that is unlucky – and then home in on that target.

So by moving rapidly and unpredictably in sync with the others in the flock, each individual – and the flock as a whole – confuses the attacker, and gives the bird a chance to evade capture. One Boxing Day a few years ago I watched up to four peregrines above the murmuration, each seeking out a suitable target. None of them succeeded in catching and killing a starling, and in my experience, they rarely do.

In 2008, a group of Italian scientists from the University of Rome tested an interesting hypothesis: that the specific way in which starlings flock together is directly related to the risk of predation. They did so by studying two urban roosts in Rome, one of which regularly attracted peregrines, the other seeing far fewer peregrine–starling encounters.

We predicted that the higher predation pressure in one of the roosts would be reflected in larger and more compact flocks, thought to be less vulnerable to predation than small flocks.

To their delight, the theory was proved correct:

Significantly higher frequencies of compact and large flocks were observed in the roost with high predation pressure, while small flocks and singletons were more frequent at the roost with low predation pressure.

Ironically, however, they also discovered that the peregrines were, on average, more successful at making kills at the second roost, where predators were present less frequently. This suggested that the more intense flocking behaviour was effective in reducing successful predation, despite predation pressure actually being higher. That may have been because the starlings at the less-predated roost were lulled into a false sense of security, or because they had less experience at evading predators.

In a later study, published in 2014, the same scientists went one step further. They exposed adult starlings to a video showing a flock being attacked by a peregrine, to discover whether this experience would affect their subsequent behaviour. Surprisingly, perhaps, it did:

> The video of the flock under attack caused an increase in immobility and vigilance, more marked in singletons, both during and after the exposure . . . The results are in line with previous field studies, which showed that isolated starlings are exposed to a higher risk of predation compared to individuals in flocks.

When it comes to the other theory about why starlings gather in such numbers – their need to stay warm during cold winter nights – the verdict is less clear-cut. While it might appear to make sense that larger gatherings keep the birds warmer, the evidence is not that compelling.

Professor Anne Goodenough of the University of Gloucestershire has studied no fewer than 3,000 starling murmurations, and discovered that there is little or no correlation between the air temperature and the size of the displays, whereas if keeping warm were a key factor you would expect that the colder it gets, the larger the gatherings would be.

This suggests that although keeping warm might be a useful side benefit, the main reason for the gatherings – and especially for the aerial displays before going to roost – is to avoid being picked off by a predator.

The second question I am often asked is this: how on earth do the murmurating starlings manage to perform such complex aerial displays without bumping into one another? As we stand and watch in open-mouthed awe, it is hard to understand why they do not. But once again scientists have tried to answer this, by constructing complex mathematical models to test their theories.

Over time, birds have evolved all sorts of clever strategies to avoid problems such as collisions and, like all evolutionary developments, these skills have been honed over countless generations. But it wasn't until 2016 that a group of scientists at Queensland University in Australia worked out exactly how they actually do it.

In what was dubbed 'the Flyway Code', they found that when two birds fly towards each other, with a growing risk of a collision, each bird takes evasive action by veering away: not randomly, but always in a specific direction. As Professor Mandyam Srinivasan, who led the research, explained:

> Birds must have been under strong evolutionary pressure to establish basic rules and strategies to minimise the risk of collision in advance . . . Our modelling has shown that birds always veer right – and sometimes they change their altitude as well, according to some pre-set preference.

As Professor Srinivasan also noted, these findings might now help us to avoid human collisions, notably the most disastrous of all, between two aircraft:

As air traffic becomes increasing busy, there is a pressing need for robust automatic systems for manned and unmanned aircraft, so there are real lessons to be learned from nature.

But what strategy do the birds use when they are in the middle of a huge, constantly moving flock? Again, scientists – this time based at Princeton University in the United States – think they have found the answer: the power of seven. To be more specific, each bird needs to keep a close eye on its nearest seven neighbours, and try – if it can – to remain equidistant from them. So a sudden movement from any one bird will trigger a ripple effect through the rest of the flock, as the other birds respond.

To be honest, this is not something of which I – or any other observer on the ground – have ever been aware. No matter how closely we watch a murmuration, the overall impression is of a kind of organised chaos, with the overall movements and changing shape of the flock as a whole making it impossible to focus on a single bird and its small cohort of near neighbours.

Nevertheless, seven appears to be the optimum number of other birds on which each individual starling is able to focus while in the centre of the murmuration, with the least expense of extra energy. Any fewer, and they might still collide; any more, and they will struggle to process the information they need.

Once again there is a useful lesson for humans in avoiding collisions, especially those taking place in fluid and uncertain environments, such as driving on motorways during rain or fog. And it doesn't get much more fluid and uncertain than the middle of a starling murmuration. As the university's research leader Naomi Leonard, Professor of Mechanical and Aerospace Engineering, noted:

In a flock with 1,200 birds, it is clear that not every bird will be able to keep track of the other 1,199 birds, so an important question is, 'Who is keeping track of whom?'

As we can see, a starling murmuration is an exceedingly complex phenomenon. And even once the birds are safely ensconced in the roost itself, that complexity continues. We might suppose that the arrangement of birds within the roost is more or less random, but nothing could be further from the truth.

There is a clear hierarchy, with adult males grabbing the best – and safest – places at the centre of the roost, and adult females and younger males further out. Young females are forced to the periphery, making them more vulnerable to being picked off by predators – which at the Avalon Marshes roost include the bitterns that now make their home here.

Indeed, during the two very cold and icy winters of 2009–10 and 2010–11, when overnight temperatures dropped below freezing for days on end, and wetlands regularly froze over, we expected that the new and very vulnerable population of bitterns would take a huge hit. Instead, their numbers continued to rise, year on year – because they found a valuable alternative food resource in the roosting starlings, which they patiently picked off by walking through the reed bed after dark.

We tend to think of 'starling tourism' – either in person or via the television or the World Wide Web – as a very modern phenomenon. Yet as long ago as the 1830s Edward Stanley was writing about a roost he regularly visited at Lymm Dam, an artificial lake near his Cheshire home. Almost two centuries ago this gathering had become a major attraction for local people.

This dam, on the finer evenings of November, was once the favourite resort of many persons, who found an additional attraction in watching the gradual assemblage of the starlings.

In a passage that could almost have been written today, Stanley went on to describe the build-up of the nightly murmurations:

About an hour before sunset, little flocks, by twenties or fifties, kept gradually dropping in, their numbers increasing as daylight waned, till one vast flight was formed, amounting to thousands, and at times we might almost say to millions . . . At first they might be seen advancing high into the air, like a dark cloud, which in an instant, as if by magic, became almost invisible, the whole body, by some mysterious watch-word or signal, changing their course, and presenting their wings to view edgeways.

Even then, long before the advances of modern industrial farming devastated the starlings' food supply, Stanley noted that their numbers were in decline.

It has been remarked, that the flights of these birds have of later years much diminished, a fact to which we can speak from our own experience, for the assemblages which we have just described . . . have long ago ceased; and it is now a rare thing to see a passing flock of even fifty, where, in years gone by, they mustered in myriads.

It is hard to see why starlings should have declined at this time, but they clearly did. In *The Historical Atlas of Breeding Birds in Britain and Ireland, 1875–1900*, Simon Holloway does note that around the time Stanley was writing the starling had become rather scarce in northern England, and indeed elsewhere.

In the first half of the [nineteenth] century it was absent from much of SW England, W Wales, the mainland of Scotland north of the Forth/Clyde valley and W Ireland. It was rare, too, at this time in N England.

Towards the end of the century, however, numbers had bounced back, and starlings' roosts had again become a visitor attraction, as W. H. Hudson reported in his popular 1895 book *British Birds*:

In a district where they are abundant, they are seen at the end of each day gathering from all directions to the roosting-place; and it is then that the 'cloud of starlings' may be seen at its best, and it is certainly one of the finest sights that birdlife presents in England.

Just over fifty years later, in *London's Birds* (1949), Richard Fitter provided the first detailed and authoritative account of starlings roosting on urban buildings, displaying his knowledge of classical architecture in the process:

Anyone who is familiar only with the huge congregations of starlings in country thickets and reedbeds may be surprised at the suggestion that the roosting of starlings on buildings in our larger cities is not quite a new departure . . . In London starlings now roost on ledges of buildings all over the central district, and show an especial liking for the acanthus leaves of Corinthian capitals [a phenomenon originally noticed by his contemporary Max Nicholson].

As Fitter noted, this was a relatively recent phenomenon: starlings had only been roosting in urban areas for just over fifty years. Several writers from the early 1890s regarded the starling as purely a breeding bird in London, which 'nested in tree-holes in the parks and departed for the country at the end of the summer'. The appearance of large and noisy flocks in winter even gave rise to a lengthy series of letters to the *Times* newspaper, in which one correspondent boasted that when he fired a shotgun at the massing birds, he could hit a dozen at a time.

By 1898 Hudson had observed them roosting in four London parks – St James's, Regent's, Battersea and around the Serpentine in Hyde Park – at least from late June to October, although frustratingly he does not say whether they then stayed put for the whole of the winter.

But by 1900 we know they were roosting in the extensive grounds of Buckingham Palace during the month of February, where they had more than likely been present throughout the winter months.

During the years before the First World War a starling roost was also observed by the naturalist Julian Huxley outside his home in Westbourne Square, just north of Hyde Park. He must have mentioned this to his brother Aldous, whose novel *Antic Hay*, published in 1923, features a character who 'looked on the regular nightly visitation of the starlings as a token of stability in the turbulent world of the twenties'.

By the winter of 1919–20 the shooting editor of the *Field*, Eric Parker, reported hordes of starlings roosting on the British Museum in Bloomsbury, as well as on St Paul's Cathedral, and commented that they had not been at either site before the First World War. By 1922 they were roosting on buildings all over central London.

T. S. Hawkins' book *The Soul of an Animal* (1921) includes a letter to the *Morning Post* newspaper that describes the annual congregation of starlings in the plane trees at London's Temple as though it were a meeting of humans:

> Year after year they gather in the middle of September, and sometimes they have resolutions and amendments which cause the meeting to be adjourned for a couple of days.

Other writers of the day used similarly anthropomorphic language to describe the roosts. The poet Edmund Blunden wrote of them 'each flying to his mansion overhead . . . through maelstrom roars and wild light volleys vast, each calm and glad abed', while the nature writer H. J. Massingham set down in rather intense, purple prose his observations of the starling roost on an island (actually a peninsula) in St

James's Park, with an interesting reference to what was then the very recent phenomenon of wildlife films:

> They straggle overhead in ones and twos, in small detachments and in loose hordes. They troop in mostly from west and south-west and for nearly two hours until the trees and creepers of the Island bear their black plums as rapidly as though speeded up on a nature film. The even-song swells tidally until it crisps over the human perambulants in subdued wavelets.

All these early-twentieth-century roosts were in trees, rather than on buildings. The first account Richard Fitter found of the birds roosting on a specifically man-made structure came from 1914, when they were seen landing on Nelson's Column in Trafalgar Square; three years later the same observer saw large numbers of them gathering around the Houses of Parliament.

Several decades later, on the surprisingly early date of 12 August 1949, a large, pre-roost gathering of starlings perched on the minute hand of the clock of Big Ben (strictly speaking the name of the bell rather than the tower itself), which temporarily brought the mechanism to a halt for a few minutes. This inevitably led to calls in Parliament for the birds to be culled.

A few years afterwards, in August 1954, the comedy quartet of Spike Milligan, Harry Secombe, Peter Sellers and Michael Bentine devoted an entire episode of the popular BBC Radio series *The Goon Show*, 'The Starlings', to how to rid London of these pesky birds. The script was a classic example of the Goons' offbeat and often surreal humour:

> 1954: a world overshadowed by doubts, fears, uncertainty . . . At this moment the House of Commons are debating serious matters . . . 'There are far too many starlings in Trafalgar Square (Hear, hear). We must get rid of these disgusting creatures . . .'

The episode goes on to describe the methods used to disperse the birds:

> The inventive genius of the country was called upon, and for three years the starlings were attacked with a series of frightening devices: 'stuffed owls, wriggling rubber snakes, high-frequency sound beams . . . rice puddings fired from catapults, recording of a female starling in trouble, recording of a female starling not in trouble . . .' For some inexplicable reason, all these devices failed; the starlings remained.

This curious programme, whose humour, it must be said, has not aged well, ends with the drastic use of 'explodable birdlime', launched by HM the Queen, which initially succeeds in driving the starlings away, but also results in the destruction of St Martin-in-the-Fields, Trafalgar Square.

Comedy aside, the large numbers of roosting starlings did cause genuine problems. In the first volume of his epic, twelve-part series *The Birds of the British Isles*, published in 1953, the ornithologist David Bannerman noted that the starling is 'a bird which has increased enormously in numbers in these islands and in some districts has become almost a plague . . . This is particularly so in the London area, where incredible numbers come to roost every evening in the public parks and on buildings, from which it is impossible to dislodge them.'

As he went on to explain, in compelling detail,

> The birds travel long distances to these roosts, and afford a familiar sight to Londoners as flock after flock wing their way over house-tops with fast direct flight until, when reaching the rendezvous, they literally rain down upon the trees, which soon become so full that it seems not one more can get a footing – and still they come, settling in the topmost branches with much commotion and chatter.

As recently as the early 1980s, on occasional visits to central London, I remember seeing huge gatherings each winter's evening around London's Leicester Square. They would fly in at dusk and, once they landed, made an incredible racket, which even the gathering theatregoers noticed. Indeed, it is said that visitors to this London landmark were advised to carry a copy of the *Evening Standard* newspaper and hold it above their heads to avoid being spattered by the birds' copious droppings. Other newspapers were presumably just as effective.

During this same period there were smaller roosts on structures in other parts of London, including a well-visited one on Battersea Bridge across the River Thames. I also recall seeing flocks gathering in their thousands about that time to roost on the roof of Bristol's Temple Meads railway station – that impressive Victorian structure of metal and glass designed by Isambard Kingdom Brunel.

Virtually all these urban roosts are long gone. This is partly because from the mid-1980s onwards, as Andrew Self records in *The Birds of London* (2014), the authorities began to take specific action to discourage starlings, in order to reduce or prevent the damage their nightly deposits were doing to stonework and parked cars, and the potential danger to passers-by of slippery droppings deposited on the pavements below.

However, as Self goes on to report, the methods used – banging dustbin lids or playing distress calls to scare the birds – were largely ineffective. It appears that the roosts eventually disappeared of their own accord, following a major decline in the numbers of starlings arriving and wintering in the UK:

> Since the beginning of the twenty-first century the largest roost count [in the whole of the London area] has not exceeded 5,000 birds, and the spectacle of watching flight lines heading into town has ended.

The disappearance of starlings from their urban roosts is not just confined to London. Writing in the BTO journal *Bird Study* in 1967, the ecologist Dr G. R. (Dick) Potts suggested that a total of 39 UK cities used to support almost 70 urban roosts; today, they've nearly all gone, thanks to the worrying fall in numbers, which the BTO's own research has verified.

Although the fieldwork for the BTO's *Bird Atlas 2007–11* took place well over a decade ago, it remains the most recent full national survey of our breeding and wintering bird distribution. According to the *Atlas*, 'with the exception of the highest ground in northern and western Scotland, starlings are widespread throughout Britain and Ireland,' being found in

92 per cent of more than 3,800 10-kilometre squares surveyed. However, although this is only marginally lower than the 96 per cent of squares occupied in the original 1968–72 *Atlas*, the detailed abundance maps in this latest volume tell a very different story. Over a period of just fifteen years, from 1995 to 2010, starling numbers breeding in Britain fell by *half*. Indeed, since I was a fledgling birder in the mid-1970s, they have dropped by two-thirds – one of the most rapid declines of any British bird.

As a result, in 2002 the species was added to the UK Red List of Birds of Conservation Concern. And, just like another once common and often overlooked bird, the house sparrow, it remains there to this day.

This precipitous decline is mainly the result of the starling's reduced breeding success. We used to expect that roughly one in three juvenile starlings would reach their first birthday; today that figure has more than halved, to just 15 per cent – fewer than one in six.

As with so many recent falls in bird populations, the main reason is a lack of food, caused by agricultural intensification. Starlings feed mainly on soil invertebrates, especially leatherjackets (the larvae of the crane fly). The ubiquitous use of chemicals on our lowland grasslands combines with an increased frequency of hot, dry summers brought about by the climate crisis in a double whammy on leatherjacket numbers and, as a direct consequence, for starlings.

Chris Feare suggests that starlings have also suffered from the widespread replacement of grassland by arable crops, the often indiscriminate use of pesticides (especially ivermectin, an anti-parasitic drug which, when given to cattle, pigs and horses, reduces the availability of insects and their larvae in their droppings), and the increase in autumn sowing of cereal crops, which deprives starlings and other farmland birds of the seeds on which they feed during the winter months.

The starling has undergone a parallel decline – for much the same reasons – across much of western Europe, which has in turn led to a reduction in wintering populations across Britain. Yet it seems to be holding its own, or even increasing, in central, eastern and southern Europe. That's because there, agricultural intensification has not been so rapid, or so environmentally disastrous, as here – at least, not yet. It's led to the most spectacular winter murmurations anywhere in Europe, in the heart of Rome, creating huge environmental problems for that city and its ancient buildings.

I said that today 'virtually all' urban roosts have gone, yet starlings do sometimes still gather in urban areas, though not on buildings, as they did in the past. As well as the famous roosts on Aberystwyth and Brighton Piers, they can also turn up in the most unexpected places. In late 2023, Dr Jessica Tipton of the Natural History Museum posted a dramatic video on the social media platform X (formerly Twitter), with the caption,

Sound up! Wow! Dozens of starlings roosting in shopping centre amidst noisy traffic, dazzling lights and shoppers (some stopped to see what was going on).

This took place on a Saturday evening in early October, at the Lexicon, a shopping centre in the town of Bracknell. Described as 'Berkshire's leading shopping destination', and 'the perfect place to shop, dine and socialise', it also turns out to be attractive to Britain's most sociable bird.

At first, as Jessica headed back to her car loaded down with shopping, she assumed that the cacophony she was hearing from the adjacent hedge was a tape of 'nature noises' being played through speakers as some attempt of mitigation for this urban development. But as she got closer, and the volume increased, she soon realised this was the genuine sound of thousands of starlings gathering to roost:

> Traffic, families and teenagers with their bags of shopping, were all coming past as it got dark, some stopping to see what the racket was.

Using her Merlin birdsong app to confirm her initial identification, Jessica then caught sight of them. She stayed until after dusk, using her smartphone to video and record the event. Having spent part of her life in Glastonbury, she told me that she really misses the starling murmurations on Somerset's Avalon Marshes:

> But this experience showed you can enjoy these spectacles in an urban setting, a brilliant example of wildlife seizing the opportunity of a few protective bushes in a sprawling Bracknell retail complex.

But without doubt the most fascinating – and truly bizarre – description of starling murmurations dates back more than four centuries, to autumn 1621. The events took place in Cork, in south-west Ireland, and were preserved for posterity by an anonymous chronicler who the following year published a slender pamphlet with the intriguing title, 'The Wonderfull Battell of Starelings, fought at the Citie of Corke in Ireland, the 12. and 14. of October, 1621'.

The pamphlet's author describes how in early October that year 'an unusual multitude of birds called Stares, in some Countries knowne by the name of Starlings . . . mustered together', having arrived in the city from the east and west. On the Friday or Saturday morning the battle commenced.

> Upon a strange sound and noise made as well on the one side as on the other, they forthwith at one instant took wing, and so mounting up into the skies, encountered one another, with such a terrible shock, as the sound amazed the whole city and all the beholders.

As the author goes on to reveal, this was no ordinary murmuration, but something more akin to open warfare, with unfortunate and rather grisly consequences for the birds:

> Upon this sudden and fierce encounter, there fell down into the city, and into the Rivers, multitudes of Starlings . . . some with wings broken, some with legs and necks broken, some with eyes picked out, some their bills thrust into the breasts & sides of their adversaries, in so strange a manner, that it were incredible except it were confirmed by letters of credit, and by eye-witnesses, with that assurance which is without all exception. [I have modernised the spelling for easier reading].

There then followed a lull for a day or two, after which, on the Monday, the birds returned for a final, decisive battle, resulting in even more dead birds falling from the sky onto the city streets – as graphically illustrated on the pamphlet's cover.

To the modern reader this account seems utterly far-fetched, but we must remember that our seventeenth-century ancestors had very different belief-systems from ours. Science was in its infancy, profound

religious beliefs and ancient superstitions dominated daily life, and God was not some abstract, other-worldly deity but one who regularly intervened in, and shaped, people's lives.

The historian Dr Laura Sangha of the University of Exeter, to whom I am indebted for drawing my attention to this fascinating story, notes that, far from this account being unusual, it is fairly typical of its time. The idea of 'strange events' which were subsequently interpreted as a message from God was a common phenomenon, as another historian of the period, Professor Alexandra Walsham of the University of Cambridge, confirms. People of this period, Dr Sangha suggests, would have seen God's intervention in the world to create an unnatural event (i.e. birds aping human military activity), as a religious message, revealing divine providence. A ballad composed soon after the 'battle' confirms her interpretation:

At Corke in Ireland, where with might and maine,

they fought together till scores of them were slaine,

their fight began and ended with such hate,

some strange event it did prognosticate.

It's most likely, says Dr Sangha, that what the people of Cork had witnessed was simply a starling murmuration – perhaps rather larger than usual – but nevertheless a purely natural event that was then reinterpreted through religious eyes.

Although it is not explicitly mentioned in the account, it is also likely that those starlings were attacked by a predator. That would fit in with a moment that occurs about halfway through the famous 'Murmuration' video posted by Liberty Smith and Sophie Windsor Clive on YouTube, when something very dramatic happens. The birds, which until then have been gradually gathering in loose flocks in the skies above the filmmakers' heads, suddenly move much closer together, in a spectacularly tight and intense formation. What is not visible from the video is a predator – almost certainly a peregrine – creating a sense of panic which then runs through the entire flock.

The starlings' response is more complex than it might first appear. As Charlotte Hemelrijk of the University of Groningen in the Netherlands revealed in her 2015 paper 'Waves of terror in starling flocks', flocks of starlings under attack from a predator do not simply respond by becoming tighter and more close-knit. They also show what she calls an 'agitation wave'. This can be seen by human observers in the form of a dark pattern appearing to pass rapidly through the flock from one side to another, without this necessarily changing its shape or size.

The agitation wave can be explained by the action of individual birds within the flock as a whole: as the predator approaches, they engage in a zigzag manoeuvre, rolling from one side to another, thereby temporarily revealing their larger and darker wing surface, which accounts for the dark pattern we can momentarily see.

As Dr Hemelrijk points out, similar changes in shade and pattern – notably a flash from light to dark and back again – can also be observed in tight flocks of waders such as dunlins, when they are being pursued by a peregrine or merlin, an event I have often observed at high tide on winter days over the Parrett estuary near my home.

This might explain the scenes witnessed in Cork and described in the 'Battle of Starlings' pamphlet. But it doesn't account for the description of the birds falling out of the sky and dying on the city streets. One or two might be killed by a predator, of course, but surely not 'multitudes'.

The story of some kind of avian massacre might of course be exaggeration or invention on the part of the anonymous author, who admits he did not witness the battle himself and has had to rely on eyewitness accounts from secondary sources. But might it perhaps be explained by a curious – and initially inexplicable – event that took place recently on the island of Anglesey in North Wales?

Shortly before sunset, on the afternoon of 10 December 2019, a member of the public reported finding the fresh corpses of more than 220 starlings spread out on a 100-metre stretch of a narrow country road near the village of Bodedern, in the west of the island. Many more were found dead in the hedgerows immediately to the side of the road.

At first officers from North Wales police's rural crime team described the mass deaths as a mystery, with a strong suspicion that the starlings might have been accidentally or deliberately poisoned. To check this hypothesis they called in the Welsh government's animal and plant health agency to examine the specimens more closely.

But after carrying out post-mortems, which found no trace of any harmful substances or disease, but did find severe internal injuries, the investigators came to a very different conclusion. They suggested that the birds had simply flown straight down onto the surface of the road, and died instantly from the trauma of the impact. As Rob Taylor from the rural crime team announced on Twitter,

> The trauma supports the case that the birds died from impact with the road. It's highly likely the murmuration took avoiding action whilst airborne, from possibly a bird of prey [again, probably a peregrine], with the rear of the group not pulling up in time and striking the ground.

Dr Sangha alerted me to another, very similar phenomenon from the city of Cuauhtémoc, in northern Mexico, which took place on the morning of 7 February 2022. A video from a security camera, which accompanies the report in the *Guardian* newspaper, shows a flock of hundreds of yellow-headed blackbirds concentrating into a dark shape and then literally falling out of the sky, with many crashing onto the road and pavement below, where they were instantly killed by the impact.

Initially a local vet suggested this was caused by a combination of pollution from wood-burning stoves and the cold winter weather, while conspiracy theorists on social media predictably blamed the installation of 5G technology. However, Dr Richard Broughton, a British ecologist who analysed the footage, was sure that – just as in the Anglesey incident – the panic was caused by an unseen predator, which had forced the flock to concentrate so tightly that birds at the bottom could not take evasive action, and were pushed down to the ground.

Dr Alexander Lees, a senior lecturer in conservation biology at Manchester Metropolitan University, agrees with this verdict:

> I'd say the most probable cause is the flock murmurating to avoid a predatory raptor and hitting the ground. There always seems to be a knee-jerk response to blame environmental pollutants, but . . . in a tightly packed flock, the birds are following the movements of the bird in front rather than actually interpreting their wider surroundings, so it isn't unexpected that such events happen occasionally.

Could the huge murmurations reported in October 1621 over the city of Cork perhaps have been disturbed by a predator, leading them to panic and try to escape, with some consequently crashing into the ground? As a reason for the curious events of that time this may ruin the mystery for some, yet for me it does seem to be the most likely explanation.

Perhaps the best-known starling murmuration – and certainly the most frequently viewed on TV – is one that took place above a wooded valley alongside the River Severn in Gloucestershire, and featured in the BBC TV series *Bill Oddie's How to Watch Wildlife*, filmed in November 2004 and broadcast in early 2005. Years later, Bill and I were doing a two-man show at the City Varieties Music Hall in Leeds, during which we showed clips from the various series that we had made together, in Britain and around the world. We had saved the starling murmuration until last: as Bill explained, it was our equivalent of the Beatles' 'Hey Jude' (although he didn't persuade the audience to sing along).

Watching the clip again almost twenty years after it was filmed, I am struck by two things – both relating to the soundtrack. First, the editor used an instrumental from the jazz fusion pianist Keith Jarrett, which works surprisingly well. That cannot be said for the contribution from the dubbing mixer, who decided the music wasn't quite dramatic enough and added the sound of chattering starlings. Unfortunately he did so not once the birds had landed, but while they were still in flight – not realising that murmurating starlings don't actually call while they are still in the air.

Nevertheless, the sequence is, thanks to Bill's whispered description of the whole event, and his use of an imaginary baton to conduct the aerial movements, utterly magical. As he – and we – watch the starlings flocking together above his head, he observes that as they get lower and lower it feels as if the ceiling is coming down on top of him.

Then, as they finally drop down to roost, he explains why this is such a special event to witness:

> Just watch how these shapes change; and it's almost like it's intentional, as if there's a leader up there . . . Heaven knows how many are here now.

> I haven't a clue – there could be half a million . . . and down they go,
> cascading down . . . the waterfall.

The notes accompanying this clip on the BBC website told me something I was previously unaware of. Apparently just before the shoot the flock had disappeared from its usual site at the Wildfowl and Wetlands Trust headquarters at Slimbridge.

> After several days of doggedly tracking every small group of starlings,
> the crew discovered the entire flock minutes down the road. Local
> observers confirmed that the birds took an annual 'holiday' in the nearby
> reed bed before returning to their usual winter roost.

The sequence proved so memorable that a few years later we received a request from an advertising agency, offering a tidy sum (to the BBC, not me) to use the clip in a TV advert. Soon afterwards, 30 seconds of murmurating starlings (without Bill) appeared on prime-time ITV. The footage was set to the soundtrack of the 2005 song 'Living for the Weekend' by the English indie band Hard-Fi, and ended with the word 'BELONG' in the style of the logo of a famous brand of lager. As Bill mischievously observed, referring to a rival beer brand, starlings really do refresh the parts other birds cannot reach!

While we are on the subject of lager, there are just two pubs in Britain with 'Starling' in their name. They are the Starling, Harrogate (which styles itself an 'Independent Bar Café Kitchen') and the Starling Cloud in the Welsh seaside town of Aberystwyth, where on winter evenings hordes of starlings still gather to roost on the town's pier. Chris Feare tells me there used to be a third, also called the Starling, in the north-west London suburb of Pinner, but sadly, like so many other traditional pub names, this was lost to posterity in 2011 when the pub was rebranded with the appallingly trendy and utterly meaningless name Sync.

John Lawton's fascinating account of avian pub names, *Inn Search of Birds: Pubs, People and Places* (2023), notes that

> the Starling Cloud . . . has a lovely sign showing a single starling in the foreground and a murmuration in the background; there's a 3D wall sculpture of a murmuration on the pub itself.

Lawton goes on to say that although the Starling in Harrogate has no birds depicted on its sign, its website does explain the rather unusual choice of name.

> On the face of it a drab little bird just like any other. But to see them flying together in a flock inches from each others' wings more intricately and aerobatically than the Red Arrows . . . you are blown away by the awesome capabilities of this little bird. Its true magic only evident when flying as part of a community, a team. Those values are the backbone of our vision and goals too.

To me, this feels like a less cynical, and more genuine, version of that lager advert, and shows that although many people still feel rather ambivalent about starlings, others have taken this bird to their hearts.

One question that interests me as a student of English is the development over time of the word 'murmuration'. The *Oxford English Dictionary* first cites the word – though with a very different meaning – from as long ago as the late fourteenth century, more or less exactly contemporary with Geoffrey Chaucer's *Canterbury Tales*:

murmuration, n.

The action of murmuring; the continuous utterance of low, barely audible
sounds; complaining, grumbling; an instance of this. Now chiefly literary.

It took another two centuries or so – to William Shakespeare's era –
for the first reference in the *OED* to the modern, bird-related meaning.
It appears as 'A murmuration of Stares' in Thomas Snodham's 1614
work *A Jewell for Gentrie*, whose subtitle describes it as 'an Exact Dictionary, or True Method, to make any Man understand all the Art,
Secrets, and Worthy Knowledges belonging to Hawking, Hunting,
Fowling and Fishing'.

One modern writer on words and language, Chloe Rhodes, includes
an even earlier reference, however, in her 2014 book *An Unkindness of
Ravens: A Book on Collective Nouns*, noting that a manuscript held in the
British Library refers to a 'murmuracyon' as long ago as 1468.

By the nineteenth century references to starling murmurations had become increasingly regular, and suggest that the noun could be used to refer to 'any assemblage of starlings', rather than just those nightly winter gatherings.

But is 'murmuration' simply a collective noun, or does it refer specifically to the rushing sound we hear as a huge flock of birds passes over our heads? 'As with many terms that describe flocks of birds,' argues Chloe Rhodes, 'this one is inspired by the sound the birds make when they're flocking together.' In his article about collective nouns in the *Independent* in 2007, the environmental writer Michael McCarthy agrees:

> A murmuration of starlings denotes in sound as well as meaning the immense, sibilant rustle of the vast starling assemblies – millions strong – that sometimes come together for nightly roosts.

I find it fascinating that despite McCarthy's justifiable fears that many collective nouns for birds are disappearing – few people nowadays, for instance, refer to 'a murder of crows', 'an unkindness of ravens' or 'an exaltation of larks' – the word murmuration is still so widely used. Moreover, it has also been applied to describe the tight, turning flocks of waders when they are being pursued by a predator; a rare example of a collective noun gaining wider use in recent times. Indeed, the *OED*'s rival, the *Cambridge Dictionary*, hedges its bets when defining the word: 'A large group of birds, usually starlings, that all fly together and change direction together, *or the act of birds doing this* [my italics].'

For the academic and author Katherine Rundell, in her award-winning 2013 work of children's fiction *Rooftoppers*, the word doesn't even need to refer to birds: 'A what-eration? A murmuration. When the sea and wind murmur in time with each other, like people laughing in

private.' The broader use of 'murmuration' in these different contexts suggests to me that the word has become more commonplace.

Just as I was coming to the end of writing this biography, I came across a book I had not encountered before, entitled *I Flew with the Birds*. Published in 1949, it was written by Harald Penrose who, the dust jacket informed me, was 'a test pilot of many years' experience', and also 'an ornithologist, [who] has made a special study of the behaviour of birds on the wing'. As Penrose himself puts it,

> When one is flying in their company they are appreciated, not as automata . . . but as vital, carefree creatures, living intensely for the moment, applying an intelligence as discriminating as ours to factors affecting their lives.

Curious, I turned to Chapter XVIII, with the intriguing title 'Massed Flight of the Starlings'. Perhaps because of Harald Penrose's military background, I expected a rather dry, fact-heavy account. Instead, to my delight, I discovered writing informed by his experience and expertise, yet also deeply thoughtful and poetic – and in its account of starling murmurations, as fine as any I have read.

The chapter begins with Penrose flying 'above the flat Shropshire fields' as the sun is setting. Anxious that the fading light will cause him problems before he lands at the aerodrome, some 40 miles away on the outskirts of Worcester, he is too busy to notice anything out of the ordinary. Fortunately, his companion is more observant:

> At that moment I was startled by the voice of my passenger, ringing clear in the earphones above the aircraft's sleepy drone. 'What a cloud of birds!' she exclaimed, and waved towards a wing-tip.

Penrose looks down, to witness how

> In a great cube, so thick that it seemed impossible to see through the mass of beating wings to the ground below them, the birds slowly obliterated first one field and then another. Though they flew at over 30 miles an hour they gave the impression of no more than drifting like a smoky cloud.

He pulls his plane upwards in a steep climb to get a better view, then has to look away to mark the location on his map. When he looks back only moments later the birds have vanished, having, as he told his companion, 'just flipped out of the air like rabbits into a burrow'.

He never saw such a sight again, at least while flying. But a few years later he did witness a similar murmuration from the ground: by the Helford River in Cornwall. Before doing a series of back-of-the-envelope calculations to try to work out the density and numbers involved, he allowed himself briefly to get carried away by the sheer spectacle of the scene:

> There was a wild whirr of wings, and starlings topped the hedge so closely they almost touched the car roof. I stopped . . . [and] saw them go tip-tilting into a straggling beech copse, 200 yards away. From south and

north, from all points of the compass, other groups were arriving. Flock and flock went diving steeply down, on half-closed wings, shooting through the ragged branches of an elder hedge and, in dense packs, dropping into an adjacent field that was loosely strewn with farmyard muck. There they restlessly paced to and fro, pecking feverishly at the choice grubs the litter provided. A vast chattering, whistling and hissing came from field, hedge and copse. And still the birds rained in, only at the latest moment checking their steep, fast descent with upraised and urgently beating wings.

I Flew with the Birds was Harald Penrose's first book, published at the comparatively advanced age of forty-five (though he had of course been rather busy during the war years). He went on to write several other books on the history of British aviation, and about his own distinguished flying career, before his death in 1996, at the age of ninety-two.

But he never quite recaptured the sheer wonder at seeing that vast flock of starlings from the air, a privilege few people have ever enjoyed; nor, in my view, has anyone captured the experience of seeing these birds quite so well.

6

THE GLOBAL STARLING

If the occupation of a large geographical range can be taken as a criterion of success, then there is no doubt that the European starling is *the* successful starling.

Christopher Feare, *The Starling* (1984)

One fine March day in 1890, a wealthy New Yorker named Eugene Schieffelin changed the course of US history. He did so not by running for political office, orchestrating a mass shooting spree or starting a war. Instead, he simply released a flock of sixty starlings, which he had brought across the Atlantic by ship from England, into New York's Central Park.

The following year, 1891, he set another forty starlings free at the same location. Within a few decades the descendants of those hundred birds had spread across the entire continent. Today the European starling, as it is known here, is one of North America's commonest birds, with an estimated 60 to 140 million individuals – somewhere between a fifth and almost half of the entire world population – even though in the past fifty years numbers have dropped substantially, perhaps by as much as half.

Starlings are found as far north as Alaska and the Canadian Yukon, as far south as central Mexico, and all the way from the Atlantic coast to the Pacific. As in their native Europe, they mainly live alongside humans, being what scientists call 'commensal', which inevitably brings them into conflict with us. As the bird artist and ornithologist David Sibley notes in his *North American Bird Guide* (2000), the starling is now 'one of the most common birds wherever human settlement occurs'.

Like other species that have been introduced – by accident or by design – into regions where they have never occurred naturally, the European starling has had a major impact, both on human society and on its fellow bird species. That is because, again like other non-natives, the starling fills a 'spare' ecological niche, one not already being exploited by native species.

In *Naturalised Birds of the World* (2005) Christopher Lever points out that the starling should have faced stiff competition from other common and widespread native American species which have also evolved to live alongside and exploit humans, such as the red-winged blackbird, common grackle and brown-headed cowbird. Yet the starling has still managed to find a vacant niche to exploit, hence its success. Chris Feare believes that it benefitted from its unique 'open-bill probing' feeding method (see Chapter 3), which rival grassland birds are unable to use, enabling the starling to better exploit invertebrates that live beneath the surface of the soil.

For North American farmers, although starlings do bring some economic benefits, notably by predating on harmful invertebrates in the soil, they also cause problems. As in Europe, they feed on a wide range of commercial crops, including fruits, berries, maize, seeds and grains, as one recent report from the US Department of Agriculture noted:

> Starlings damage apples, blueberries, cherries, figs, grapes, peaches and strawberries. Besides causing direct losses . . . starlings peck and slash at fruits, reducing product quality and increasing the fruits' susceptibility to diseases and crop pests.

Starlings also consume food intended for livestock such as cattle, and can even pick out high-protein supplements specially added to the feed, at a cost estimated back in the late 1960s of more than $80 for every thousand starlings present (potentially a far higher sum today, given the huge rise in costs since then).

One detailed study carried out at Columbia University notes that starlings don't only consume the animals' food, but also contaminate feeding and water troughs with their copious droppings, potentially spreading disease. Overall, the economic damage done by starlings to the farming industry in the United States has been estimated at $1.6 *billion* a year.

Because of their status as an invasive species – and the economic damage they cause – European starlings are (along with house sparrows) exempt from the Migratory Bird Treaty Act passed by Congress in 1918, which prohibits the taking or killing of many species of birds. US scientists have even developed a poison called Starlicide (officially known as DRC-1339), which is highly toxic to starlings (and also to gulls, rooks and some gamebirds), but apparently less harmful to other birds, mammals and domestic pets which might consume it by accident.

However, the use of this toxic chemical has caused controversy, notably as a result of an incident in the New Jersey community of Griggstown, between Philadelphia and New York, in January 2009. A local farmer had complained that flocks of starlings were eating the food intended for his beef cattle and poultry, costing him $1,500 a month. He had tried using non-lethal techniques such as noisy bird scarers, but with no success. Eventually, he persuaded federal wildlife officials to put down bins containing Starlicide – but all did not go to plan, as the *New York Times* revealed:

> They were supposed to die quietly from heart and kidney failure. Instead, thousands of dead starlings rained down on the Griggstown section of Franklin Township a week ago, startling residents.

Nearby landowners were understandably concerned at finding the birds' corpses in their backyards, fearing that the starlings might have died from a disease that could harm humans. Not surprisingly, some compared the event to scenes from the Alfred Hitchcock movie *The Birds*. Eventually, after much confusion, the real cause of death was revealed, triggering a further slew of complaints, this time from local animal rights groups.

Two years later, in early 2011, a similar incident occurred in South Dakota. Yet despite concerns, the US authorities kill more starlings, using poison, trapping and shooting, than any other species of bird: an estimated 1.7 million individuals a year.

As Christopher Lever explains, starlings have caused other serious problems for humans, especially from the tons of droppings excreted at their huge roosts, which damage buildings and can potentially spread disease. They also pose a real risk to air travellers: between 1990 and 2013 alone, starlings were implicated in over 3,200 bird strikes to military and civilian aircraft, at a total cost of $7 million, although fortunately without any human fatalities. Michael Begier, National Co-ordinator for the US Department of Agriculture (USDA) Airports Wildlife Hazards Program, is no fan of the birds, because as well as gathering in large, tight flocks, they are also noticeably heavier than other birds of a similar size. As he says, 'Starlings are lean and mean. In the industry they're often called feathered bullets.'

On one disastrous occasion, on 4 October 1960, a collision with starlings did prove fatal. Soon after taking off from Boston's Logan International Airport, a Lockheed Electra commercial aircraft, Eastern Air Lines Flight 375, crashed into the nearby harbour. The aircraft immediately sank: sixty-two out of the seventy-two passengers and crew were killed, while all but one of the survivors was seriously injured. A subsequent flight investigation revealed that the aircraft had flown through a flock of starlings as it took off, with the birds sucked into all four of the turboprop engines, which immediately failed. As a result of the crash, the design of these engines was modified to prevent them ingesting birds in any future incidents. This remains the greatest loss of life from a bird strike ever recorded, anywhere in the world.

The European starling also has potentially serious impacts on North America's birdlife. As hole-nesting birds, starlings are thought to compete for breeding sites with native North American species such as sapsuckers (a kind of woodpecker). However, scientists have questioned whether they really do have an adverse effect on bird populations, as some studies have failed to show any long-term reductions.

For example, zoologist Walt Koenig's 2003 paper 'European Starlings and Their Effect on Native Cavity-Nesting Birds' concludes that although starlings do take over the nests of other birds, this may not result in significant long-term harm in the form of reduced populations of those species. This also raises a wider question about our generally negative attitudes towards invasive birds, as Koenig himself concludes:

> These results call into question our ability to predict the effects of exotic species on native species. Despite their rapid spread, striking abundance, and aggressive nature, starlings appear thus far to have had little negative effect on the native cavity-nesting bird species with which they are known to interfere.

Nevertheless, the reputation of starlings has led them to become a 'pantomime villain': in the words of one historian, 'Starlings have become some of the most reviled birds in North America.' And, given this litany of negative consequences of their presence, the blame has been placed squarely on Eugene Schieffelin himself. As one popular website noted, on 29 January 2020 (the 193rd anniversary of Schieffelin's birth),

We have celebrated the birthdays of quite a variety of people in this space, most of them brilliant or clever or industrious or otherwise admirable, and a few who had measurable shortcomings, but I dare say we have never featured anyone who arouses as much derision and distaste from Americans as Mr. Schieffelin.

Over the years, Schieffelin's motives for releasing the starlings have turned from legend into accepted fact. Almost every book, article or website that mentions the story states that his masterplan was to introduce every species of bird mentioned in Shakespeare into North America – even though the starling qualified as a result of just one reference: that brief remark by Hotspur in the history play *King Henry IV* (see Chapter 2). Even famous writers are not immune. In his informal history of American English, *Made in America* (1994), Bill Bryson writes,

> The starling . . . was brought to America by one Eugene Schieffelin, a wealthy *German emigrant* [my italics] who had the odd, and in the case of starlings regrettable, idea that he should introduce to the American landscape all the birds mentioned in the writings of Shakespeare.

In recent years, however, doubt has been cast on this beguiling tale, which suggests it is actually no more than an early example of an urban myth: a familiar and oft-repeated story, which its hearers are so inclined to believe that it eventually gains the status of undisputed fact. But before I investigate these claims, let us learn more about the man at the centre of this intriguing story, and why he might have wanted to release the starlings into Central Park in the first place.

Eugene Schieffelin has been variously described as a wealthy socialite, an eccentric drug manufacturer, a pharmacist and an amateur ornithologist. However, he was not, as Bryson and others have stated, 'a German emigrant', but a native New Yorker. Born in January 1827, he was the seventh son – and the youngest of eleven children – of Henry Schieffelin, a rich and successful New York businessman and lawyer; theirs was one of the oldest and most socially influential families in Manhattan.

In 1877 Eugene became chairman of the American Acclimatization Society. This had been founded in New York City in 1871, with the aim of bringing various species of fauna and flora to North America, by introducing 'such foreign varieties of the animal and vegetable kingdom as may be *useful or interesting* [my italics]'. At that time, the negative ecological impacts of releasing non-native species into the wild were not at all well understood, and indeed the work of these organisations was broadly given scientific backing and support.

STARLING.

With the benefit of hindsight we can now see that the acclimatisation societies caused far more harm than good. This is particularly true of regions with more specialised and pristine ecosystems, notably Australia and New Zealand, and some Pacific islands, though perhaps less so in a more varied and robust biome such as North America.

Therefore the verdict of US popular science writer Kim Todd, in her 2001 book *Tinkering with Eden: a Natural History of Exotic Species in America*, that these well-meaning endeavours resulted in ecological catastrophe, is only partly correct. She also – I think rather unfairly – describes Schieffelin as 'an eccentric at best, a lunatic at worst', and repeats, and thus gives credence to, the false myth of his Shakespearean motives.

Eugene Schieffelin died, aged seventy-nine, on 15 August 1906. During the decades after his death the story that he – with his strange Shakespearean obsession – was solely responsible for the presence of starlings in North America has been repeated and retold countless times. Yet there are two major flaws in this narrative.

The first is that his starling introductions, in 1890 and 1891, were not the first time the birds had been released into North America. In a groundbreaking paper published in 2021, entitled 'Shakespeare's Starlings: Literary History and the Fictions of Invasiveness', environmental humanists John MacNeill Miller (Allegheny College, Pennsylvania) and Lauren Fugate (Carnegie Mellon University, Pennsylvania) provide irrefutable evidence that the first releases had occurred almost two decades earlier, in the 1870s.

Another acclimatisation society, this one based in Cincinnati, Ohio, had released no fewer than 4,000 birds (though not all were starlings), while similar releases had occurred in the Canadian province of Quebec, and even (in 1877, thirteen years earlier than the notorious release by Schieffelin) in New York's Central Park.

Fugate and Miller note that previous historians acknowledged these earlier attempts, but went on to dismiss them as unsuccessful. Yet they demonstrate that several examples of small flocks of starlings were being observed in the wild in various locations during the late 1870s and 1880s, sometimes long after they were first released, suggesting that the birds were well able to survive – and indeed multiply – in their new home on the 'wrong' side of the Atlantic. As they wryly point out,

> It is true that the first successful nesting attempts observed by naturalists happened after the 1890 introduction, but that may simply register the fact that one such attempt took place beneath the eaves of the AMNH [American Museum of Natural History in New York]. As this nest was right under (or above) the noses of a full-time staff of naturalists, they could not ignore the starling's presence any longer.

Fugate and Miller then go one step further, by comprehensively debunking the myth at the very heart of the story: Schieffelin's supposed obsession with Shakespeare and his birds. In contemporary obituaries at the time of Schieffelin's death, and indeed for decades afterwards, no mention at all was made of the idea. Indeed, the very first suggestion that this was his motive didn't appear until more than fifty years after the initial releases, in *Days Without Time* (1948) a collection of natural history essays by the celebrated US naturalist Edwin Way Teale. Teale wrote that the arrival of the starling in North America 'was the result of one man's fancy', adding that '[Schieffelin's] curious hobby was the introduction into America of all the birds mentioned in the works of William Shakespeare.'

That casual, apparently off-the-cuff comment appears to be the sole source of the Shakespeare story. Even so, it did not really take hold in the American psyche for another quarter of a century. Then, in 1974, the novelist and critic Robert Cantwell published a vicious diatribe against Eugene Schieffelin, as Fugate and Miller report:

[Cantwell's article] seizes on Teale's Shakespeare claim and transforms Schieffelin into an unforgettable anti-hero . . . a crazed monomaniac, the Ahab of acclimatisation. 'He had rivals' in his efforts to introduce starlings, Cantwell claims, 'but they had no profound central purpose akin to Schieffelin's plan to import all of Shakespeare's birds, and soon gave up.'

Not content with destroying the reputation of the man, Cantwell then directed his fury at the starling itself, transforming it, in Fugate and Miller's words, 'from a well-established bird and (on balance) agricultural asset into a degenerate pest and enemy of the ecosystem'. As Cantwell wrote:

It's hard to find anyone with a kind word to say for starlings . . . Francis of Assisi, if he ever tangled with them, might have been tempted to whittle himself a slingshot.

As Fugate and Miller acknowledge, starlings are indeed a thriving, non-native species, and as such do have the potential for causing ecological, environmental and economic harm. However, they also suggest that the hysteria surrounding the presence of these birds in North America has been at least somewhat exaggerated. This clearly suits the vested interests of the agricultural industry, for whom starlings might even, says Miller, do some good:

While huge groups of starlings might be an annoyance, there's not a lot of convincing data behind the more serious economic, ecological, and epidemiological claims against these birds . . . The hatred toward starlings seems to be rooted in longstanding cultural prejudices rather than in actual facts about them.

He goes on the suggest that these prejudices might have been triggered by growing anti-immigrant sentiment in the United States:

You can see this in the very political language casting starlings as foreign invaders that appears regularly after the turn of the twentieth century.

Interestingly, this reflects attitudes towards invasive species from North America on the other side of the Atlantic, where in the United Kingdom the grey squirrel is often referred to derogatively as the 'American tree rat'. Peter Coates, Professor of American and Environmental History at the University of Bristol, shows how the British and American outlooks mirror one another, as 'the grey squirrel's misdeeds in Britain are often compared to the exploits of the uncouth and bullying "English" house sparrow and "European" starling in the USA.'

Fugate and Miller also point up this antipathy and conclude their 2021 paper with a fascinating and very apt analogy:

The Schieffelin story's plot is simple enough: like other examples of the invasive story template, it follows the contours of Mary Shelley's *Frankenstein* (1818) in tracing the disastrous effects of human hubris.

An article on the Allegheny College website quotes John MacNeill Miller in making a wider point about how culturally relative our understanding is of our own, human relationships with the natural world.

We never see nature with fresh, pure, objective eyes. We see it through the selective vision of our cultural beliefs and values . . . Being aware of our selective vision – of the way even nature is accessible to us only through the medium of culture – should remind us to be wary of perceived certainties about which animals and plants around us are 'good' and which are 'bad.' It should keep us curious and open-minded about the value of creatures we've been taught to write off as uninteresting or even insidious. Starlings probably aren't the only pest species that deserve a second look.

Today, almost a century-and-a-half after the events that began the starling's new life in North America, the tide of hatred against these European incomers might finally be on the turn. Murmurations occur there as well – many at well-known birding hotspots such as Merritt Island in Florida, Higbee Beach at Cape May in New Jersey, the Rio Grande Valley in southern Texas and the Bosque del Apache in New Mexico. In recent years, though rather later than in the UK, the US media has featured these spectacles. The usual antipathy towards the non-native starlings appears to be set aside: one report in the *San Francisco Standard* from February 2023 even provides helpful instructions for those wanting to attend, including details of where to park and what time to be there for the performance.

This new-found interest has even attracted the attention of academics. In her Stanford University blog on crowds in the works of the medieval Italian poet Dante, the American literary scholar Cynthia L. Haven includes a verse from *Inferno*, noting that 'In all the images of leaves, sand and birds, this one could easily be overlooked':

And as their wings bear the starlings along in the cold season, in wide, dense flocks, so does that blast the sinful spirits; hither, thither, downward, upward, it drives them.

As Haven admits, this made her look again at this common, much criticised and often overlooked bird:

It certainly grabbed me: my daughter, Zoë Patrick, is a 'birder', and during a recent trip to Golden Gate Park, she pointed out the drab and speckled birds . . .

The reason Dante chose starlings as a metaphor for movement is, she concludes, their extraordinary murmurations, whose impact on the observer she likens to the final line in the whole of the *Divine Comedy*: 'the Love that moves the sun and the other stars'.

Meanwhile, another US blogger, the bird scientist Zach Hutchinson from the website Flocking Around, goes even further. He recently posted 'Start Loving European Starlings', in which he robustly defended the species against its detractors, concluding, 'Love the starling for what it is: an intelligent, sirenic bird that is delightful to see as its feathers shimmer in the sunlight.'

Despite his obviously tongue-in-cheek tone, he still received hate mail in response. It seems that, despite its negative impacts being misrepresented and over-exaggerated, Americans still won't take the starling to their hearts.

Yet in 2021, a movie was released which put the species at the very centre of its narrative. *The Starling* features Melissa McCarthy and Chris O'Dowd as Lilly and Jack, a couple grieving over the sudden and unexpected death of their infant daughter. A starling nesting in their backyard initially attacks and harasses Lilly, but she gradually begins to tolerate and ultimately welcome its presence; and when the bird is injured, she nurses it back to health.

Given the traditional intolerance towards starlings in the US, this might seem an odd choice of subject, but her ambivalence towards the bird makes it an apt metaphor for dealing with her grief. Unfortunately, the film itself sank under a torrent of critical reviews. The *Guardian's* film critic Peter Bradshaw gave it one star, calling it 'staggeringly peculiar and bad', while the website Rotten Tomatoes concluded that 'Burying its talented cast and worthy themes under mounds of heavy-handed melodrama, *The Starling* is a turkey'.

North America is not the only region where starlings have been successfully (or unsuccessfully, depending on your point of view) introduced. As Christopher Lever notes, like another close associate of human beings, the house sparrow, the European starling has been highly effective in its colonisation of large swathes of the world's land-masses, including areas of Africa, Australasia and South America. Some populations, such as that in the Argentinian capital Buenos Aires, where the species was introduced in 1987, remain fairly localised, though the species is nevertheless spreading at a rate of roughly 20 kilometres a year. Elsewhere in the world starlings have moved far and wide from their original arrival point.

European starlings were brought to South Africa some time between 1897 and 1899 (probably April 1897), by the now notorious businessman and politician Cecil Rhodes. He released eighteen birds, which had been supplied by the equally infamous ornithologist and fraudster

Colonel Richard Meinertzhagen, who had in turn obtained them from a winter roost in the UK (suggesting they were probably visitors from continental Europe).

This was not long after Rhodes had resigned as Prime Minister of the Cape Colony (the western and southern parts of the country) following a disastrous military raid that eventually led to the start of the Boer War. His decision to bring these birds there from Britain turned out to be equally problematic.

Starlings soon began to spread (albeit at first fairly slowly) to other parts of the Cape. By the 1920s, they had also spread further north, into areas with fairly dense human populations. As one observer noted, 'No factor other than the occupation of human habitation is evident in the spread of the species.'

By the time of the first *South African Bird Atlas Project*, whose survey work was mainly done during the late 1980s, starlings had expanded their breeding range eastwards into much of Kwa-Zulu Natal. When the second *Bird Atlas* appeared, covering the years 2007–21, they had spread still further to the north and east, although as one observer wryly noted, 'there is still a long way to go to reach Cairo'.

However, Christopher Lever points out that the European starling may now have reached a natural limit of its range, as the species is not suited to the warmer (and less populated) regions of southern Africa, where the soil is baked too hard by the sun for the bird to be able to probe for insects with its sharp and powerful bill. The starling is likely to remain mostly confined to the western and eastern Cape, where it is one of the commonest species in towns and cities, with a population numbering in the millions. Oddly, there are also small, outlying populations in the town of Oranjemund, just across the border in Namibia, and the species is also reported to be numerous in Maseru, the capital city of landlocked Lesotho.

As in Europe and North America, starlings in South Africa have been implicated in the destruction of soft fruit crops in orchards but, as elsewhere, this may be partly compensated by their consumption of harmful insect pests. But though one observer has commented that 'Extermination rather than preservation would be favoured by most people,' he went on to add, 'there is no prospect of eliminating this resourceful bird.'

That verdict might not be accepted in another part of the world where European starlings were released even earlier than in North America and South Africa: Australia. Here the species was first introduced to Melbourne as early as 1856 or 1857, with subsequent releases, over the following decades, elsewhere in Victoria, along with parts of New South Wales, Queensland, South Australia and Tasmania.

Once again, as in North America, the acclimatisation societies (known here as committees) were the driving force behind these releases. Again, this was partly in order to import a bird familiar to homesick British settlers, but also with supposed practical aims: the starlings would, it was hoped, feed on insect pests, and also help to pollinate the flax crop.

The birds were initially encouraged by the provision of nesting boxes on farms, but they hardly needed help: by the 1920s, about half a century since the main releases, starlings had spread across much of the eastern part of the country – although by then most people regarded them as pests.

Today their range extends over a large swathe of southern and eastern Australia, including Tasmania, with the highest strongholds in the urban areas of New South Wales and Victoria. The species is usually referred to as 'common starling', as Ian Fraser and Jeannie Gray note in their guide to *Australian Bird Names*:

Certainly the commonest starling in Britain, whence comes the name. (It's also the commonest in Australia [compared with the metallic starling and introduced common myna], but that's coincidental.)

On the very first morning of my first ever visit to Australia, I came across a small flock of starlings in the Melbourne Botanical Gardens. For me, as they hopped around on the short-cropped grass among this new and exotic avifauna, accompanied by magpie-larks, Australian magpies and a pair of sulphur-crested cockatoos, they brought a strange reminder of home. Later on the same trip I saw starlings in more rural settings, near Howlong and Leeton in New South Wales, and a few years later on a subsequent visit I came across one in a remote part of rural Queensland, looking very out of place.

On a recent trip to Bruny Island, Tasmania, I was surprised at the number of times I saw starling flocks and, as I wrote in my diary, the sheer incongruity of their presence in this faraway land:

It's a bright, sunny midsummer morning. I drive down winding country lanes, past grassy fields turning from green to yellow in the summer's heat, when I notice a flock of familiar birds. Starlings – about fifty of them – perched on the telegraph wires alongside the road. Along with blackbirds, goldfinches and skylarks, their presence dominates this rural scene. But I'm not in Somerset; I'm almost 11,000 miles away from home, on the other side of the world.

But there is one part of Australia that starlings have yet to conquer: the largest state of all, Western Australia. With an area of over 2.5 million square km, if WA ever gained independence it would be the tenth largest country in the world. It is also home to one of the world's great biodiversity hotspots, known as the Southwest Australia Ecoregion, because of its very high levels of endemism, including more than 4,000 species of plants found nowhere else on the planet.

Starlings were first seen in Western Australia almost a century ago, in 1936, when a single bird was found – and 'removed' (presumably by being trapped and killed) – at Gingin, a town north of Perth. Despite their early arrival, however, they have never managed to gain a permanent foothold in the state, for two main reasons. First, the geographical barrier of the Nullabor Plain, a huge expanse of arid desert stretching across parts of Western and South Australia, acts as a natural obstacle to the species. Second, the government of Western Australia, supported by a national project, the Australian Pest Animal Strategy, has since 1971 adopted ruthless measures to hunt down and kill any starlings that do manage to cross over its borders and into the state.

To Britons, for whom culling wild species (even non-native, invasive ones) is often regarded as anathema, the brusque, ruthlessly unsentimental attitude of our Australian cousins may come as a surprise, but as the report's authors confirm,

> As an invasive pest, few bird species compare to the Common Starling (*Sturnus vulgaris*) in their ability to colonise continents, wreak havoc on many agricultural industries and adversely impact biodiversity.

The threat is certainly very real: a 2007 report recorded that during the previous thirty years no fewer 55,000 starlings had been 'removed' from the wild.

In March 2023, the Government of Western Australia issued another biosecurity alert about the common starling, reporting that several newly arrived birds had recently been reported along the south coast while, despite their best efforts, small populations of starlings are now to be found near two towns in the far south-east of the state. The alert included photographs and sound recordings of the species to enable residents to recognise, identify and report them as quickly as possible.

Sean Dooley, National Public Affairs Manager for BirdLife Australia, tells me that one potential Achilles heel in this plan is that starlings now appear to be moving along the southern coast of Australia, living on the beaches, where they can get plenty of invertebrate food thanks to the twice-daily changes along the tideline. So the jury is still out on whether the authorities will be successful in preventing one of the world's most successful birds from colonising the state permanently. But they are certainly trying as hard as they can.

The most remote and distant area of the globe where starlings can be found is New Zealand. Yet again, the birds were first brought here by those now notorious acclimatisation societies, who along with private individuals released roughly a thousand starlings from 1862 to 1883, again ostensibly in order to control insect pests – but without considering the potential problems that might result.

Initially the project was considered to be successful, and as early as 1870 – less than a decade after the first releases – the birds were already very numerous in some locations, while by the 1920s they could be found not just throughout the New Zealand mainland, but also on many offshore islands.

However, by then it was dawning on New Zealanders that the starling might not be as beneficial as they had supposed. According to Christopher Lever, these aggressive birds don't just feed on and damage many crops – especially fruit – and eat bumblebees and honeybees: they also out-compete many native bird species, including New Zealand's three endemic species of small parrots, the yellow-crowned, red-crowned and Malherbe's parakeets, for food and nest sites. This is a particular issue for Malherbe's parakeet, which, with fewer than 700 individuals remaining, is classified by BirdLife International as Critically Endangered.

More than 160 years after the starling was first brought to New Zealand, the authorities are now taking its presence very seriously indeed. A national scheme to eradicate invasive mammal species in the next two decades or so – Predator Free 2050 – has gained almost universal public support, and non-native birds might be next. So the days of the European starling in New Zealand could be numbered.

The beneficial impact of a total eradication of starlings from New Zealand is hard to overestimate. The species is now, along with the also introduced house sparrow, one of the commonest birds in the country, found not just across the whole of North and South Islands, but also well offshore, even including the sub-Antarctic archipelagos of the Snares and Antipodes.

As elsewhere, they compete with native species of bird for food and nest sites, and also feed on and damage crops. Birds from the Kermadec Islands, situated far to the north of New Zealand, may even have subsequently colonised Fiji, roughly the same distance farther north, though it is also possible that starlings were brought there separately.

Overall, starlings have not been the most popular new arrivals on their travels around the globe, though this is hardly their fault, given that they were transported by us. But the ubiquity of the European starling – just one, albeit by far the most successful, member of its family – should not stop us appreciating its many other, mostly less problematic, relatives from around the Old World.

Tourists flock to the Masai Mara in Kenya to see the three species of big cat – lion, leopard and cheetah – as well as some 'little cats' such as the serval, along with hyenas and jackals, and the 'supporting cast' of game animals alongside which the predators live and often feed. These include African elephants, giraffes and zebras, antelopes and gazelles, buffaloes and wildebeests, hippos and warthogs.

With such a globally unique concentration of mammals, both large and small, you wouldn't think birds would get much of a look-in. Yet many people I know, who initially travel to the Mara to see its famous predators and their prey, end up enthusing about the wide range of avian attractions as well. These include the magnificent African fish eagle, comical ground hornbills, and a host of colourful kingfishers, rollers and bee-eaters.

But another group of birds also demands attention: the starlings. They may not be quite as striking as those larger species, yet, as I discovered on my very first trip to the East African savannah, as producer of BBC TV's *Big Cat Diary*, their ubiquity and charismatic habits really do make them stand out, even among such a stellar cast.

On my first visit, back in 1998, I saw half-a-dozen members of the starling and myna family, including several species of glossy starlings, together with the strikingly purple and white violet-backed starling, and the curious wattled starling, the male of which has a bald patch of yellow around his eye, and long wattles hanging down from his throat. Since then, on visits to Botswana, Namibia, South Africa and Tanzania, I have added roughly another twenty starling species to my growing list.

Several, such as Cape and superb starlings, have geographical or descriptive names; others celebrate the lives of pioneering ornithologists on the African continent, including the Germans Eduard Rüppell, Johann Hildebrandt and Friedrich Meves, and Englishmen William Burchell, Gerald Waller, George Shelley and Major Reginald Watkin Edward-Kenrick. All these men (and they are all men) 'collected' (i.e. shot and killed) their eponymous birds during the nineteenth and early twentieth centuries, the high-water mark of European colonialism in Africa.

The other main centre of starling variety is Asia: more specifically the Indian subcontinent and South-east Asia, with the largest range of different species found in the forests of northern Thailand. On visits to India, Sri Lanka, Hong Kong and southern China I have seen a number of these, including the black-collared starling (one of the biggest members of its family, even larger than a mistle thrush); the strikingly handsome Brahminy starling, and a number of the common Asian species known as mynas.

According to the *Oxford English Dictionary* the name myna derives from the Hindi word *mainā*, meaning 'love'. This is a reference to the affectionate behaviour displayed between breeding pairs of the species, most easily observed when they are kept in captivity. The *OED*'s earliest written reference to the word in English comes from 1620, in a letter sent back to Britain from India, which informs the recipient that 'we have sent a cupell of pratlinge birds called mynnas'.

Mynas – also spelt 'mynahs' and sometimes rendered as 'myna bird' – are not actually a biological entity, but a cultural one. Rather than designating a specific and distinct group, the name is used for almost all members of the starling family found in the Indian subcontinent, as well as others found elsewhere in Asia. Of these, the best known are the common (or Indian) myna and the common hill myna.

The common myna inhabits a very wide range, from eastern Iran and southern Kazakhstan in the west, via southern China, India and (as a separate subspecies) Sri Lanka to the Malay Peninsula in the east, while the slightly larger common hill myna is found in north-east India and upland areas of South-east Asia. Both these birds are striking and attractive. The common myna is mainly chocolate brown, with a yellow bill and legs, a yellow marking behind each eye, and prominent white flashes in the wings, which are revealed when it flies. The hill myna is jet-black, with an orange bill, and bright yellow patches on the nape and behind the eyes. But mynas' popularity as cage birds is not down to their plumage, but rather their extraordinary skills as songsters and mimics.

Like that of the common starling, the usual song of the common myna consists of a series of grunts, croaks, whistles, clicks and chirps. And like the starling they can readily be taught to mimic other sounds, including the human voice. The common hill myna is even more remarkable as a mimic. Its natural call is a series of loud, shrill whistles that descend the musical scale, usually delivered from high in the forest canopy at dusk and dawn. But like the common starling and common myna, it has an even wider repertoire of other sounds – some musical, others not – which it learns from its parents and other birds nearby when young.

In one scientific study published in 1974, 'How does a mynah bird imitate human speech?', researchers in the United States discussed the bird's ability to accurately imitate the human voice, as well as to learn and whistle tunes played to it. The common hill myna's abilities have since been put on a par with the best-known avian imitator, the African grey parrot. As Mark Cocker noted in his comprehensive cultural over-view *Birds and People* (2013), the species 'is a good candidate for the world's most articulate bird'.

Being so accomplished, and therefore so popular as cage birds, has brought advantages and drawbacks to both these species, and also led to environmental problems. Because the common myna is so adapt-able, not least because of an omnivorous diet, the species moved into urban environments in its natural range during the past century, and has done very well there. But it has also been introduced – or escaped and established a wild breeding population – in many other parts of the world where it is not native.

These include some of the same locations as the European star-ling: South Africa, the United States, Australia and New Zealand, but also large swathes of the Arabian peninsula, including Bahrain, Kuwait, Oman, the United Arab Emirates and Saudi Arabia. There are small self-sustaining populations in Russia, Hong Kong and Japan, and the species has even bred in Spain and Italy. Could Britain be next?

The common myna has also reached more isolated locations. Having been introduced onto Ascension Island in the South Atlantic Ocean during the early nineteenth century, the species is now very common and widespread there. It is also thriving on islands in the Indian Ocean, including Diego Garcia, the Maldives and the Seychelles, where they were brought by the then governor in the 1760s. The species is now the most widespread and abundant landbird on one of the world's most remote islands, St Helena in the South Atlantic Ocean, where the entire population is thought to have descended from just five individuals released there in 1885.

With its ability to thrive in almost any tropical or warm temperate environment, from cities to remote oceanic islands, it is no wonder that the common myna is one of only three bird species on the International Union for Conservation of Nature's '100 of the World's Worst Invasive Alien Species' list, compiled in 2021, and has been dubbed 'the world's most invasive species'. (The other two, incidentally, are the red-vented bulbul, also from South-east Asia, which is causing problems on many Pacific islands, and, of course, the common starling).

Mynas do indeed cause harm: again, like the European starling, by feeding on farm crops, but also by coming into conflict with native species. In Florida, where the birds are a regular sight in shopping malls, they compete for nesting sites with purple martins, while in some locations they feed on the eggs and chicks of other birds, or aggressively chase them away from their breeding territories.

However, as with the starling, the harm these birds do might also have been somewhat exaggerated. The Global Invasive Species Database, which monitors the impact of non-native species around the world, notes that 'in India the common myna is referred to as the farmer's friend because it protects crops by feeding on insect pests'. It goes on to note that in many instances where the species was deliberately released, including to Ascension Island and the Seychelles, it was originally introduced to control insects and other invertebrates.

Being highly intelligent, the common myna has also developed what the Global Invasive Species Database calls a 'fear response; it learns about an area in which it observes another individual experience an aversive event, namely capture by a human'. Just like another successful global invader, the brown rat, mynas are what scientists call 'neophobic': in other words, they have a healthy fear of anything new or unusual in their immediate environment, and so it is very hard to eradicate them using conventional methods such as traps.

In recent years, the starling expert Chris Feare has dedicated himself to eradicating the common myna from islands in the Seychelles, where these invasive birds pose an existential threat to native bird species. He and his Seychelloise field assistant, Christine Larose, rely heavily on traps containing a live decoy bird to attract them, with the final few birds being shot by an expert marksman. As he explains, this approach has now begun to bear fruit.

> On Denis Island, the four species of endemic birds that had been introduced in small numbers to establish secure population after declines elsewhere in the archipelago, have blossomed to the extent that their conservation threat statuses have all been downgraded.

This was especially critical in the case of three of the four species, the Seychelles paradise flycatcher, Seychelles warbler and Seychelles magpie-robin, all of which had become restricted to single islands, with the magpie-robin reduced at one stage to a global population of just a dozen individuals.

From the undoubted global success of two very common and widespread starling species, the European starling and the common myna, it is easy to get the impression that all members of this large and diverse family are doing very well.

Yet, as with almost every other bird family, there is a huge gulf between the fate of the most common and successful species, and of the rarest and most endangered ones. The latter category includes several species classified by BirdLife International as of conservation concern, one of which, the Pohnpei starling, has now almost certainly become extinct.

The Pohnpei starling was discovered in the late nineteenth century, on the island of the same name, part of Micronesia, just north of the Equator in the Pacific Ocean, and one of the wettest places on the planet. Initially the species was thought to be fairly common, with no fewer than sixty specimens collected on a single expedition in the early 1930s. However, since 1956 there have only been a handful of unconfirmed sightings, and systematic expeditions in 1983 and 2010 found no evidence that any were still alive.

As with so many other oceanic island species, the likely cause of the Pohnpei starling's demise was the presence of rats. That also did for several other island races, including a starling found on Lord Howe Island, roughly 800 kilometres east-north-east of Sydney, Australia. This bird, a subspecies of the Tasman starling, was reported in 1915 as being so common it was an agricultural pest, yet, following the accidental introduction of rats from a wrecked ship in 1918, it went extinct just a few years later.

At least five other starling species, all confined to islands in the Pacific or Indian Oceans, have also gone extinct in historical times: the Rodrigues starling, Reunion starling, Kosrae starling, Norfolk Island starling (the only other race of the Tasman starling) and the aptly named mysterious starling.

The last species is indeed enigmatic: a single specimen was obtained on the island of Mauke, in the Cook Islands (between Tonga, Samoa and French Polynesia) in 1825, and the bird has never been seen – alive or dead – in the two centuries since.

Other species are also confined to a single island location. The Socotra starling, a large, glossy black bird with brick-red wing panels, is found only on the island of that name in the Arabian Sea, between Yemen and the Horn of Africa. However, despite its tiny range – Socotra is barely larger than North Yorkshire – this species is doing well, and classified by BirdLife International as being of Least Concern.

That is far from the case for another endemic island species, the Bali starling, confined to the famous tourist destination of that name in Indonesia. Also known as the Bali myna, or by its local island name *jalak Bali*, the Bali starling was first described by the German ornithologist Erwin Stresemann as recently as 1912. He initially gave it the name Rothschild's myna, after the distinguished British naturalist, collector and politician Walter Rothschild (2nd Baron Rothschild, of the famous banking family, who had no fewer than a dozen species named after him, though only one, Rothschild's swift, is still in official use).

Of all the world's starlings and mynas, the Bali starling is one of the most striking and beautiful. A little larger than our familiar European starling, it is mostly snow-white, with black tips to its wings and tail, a pale-yellow bill and a bright blue bare patch of skin around its eye, as well as a feathery crest it raises when agitated or during courtship. Unfortunately the Bali starling's good looks almost brought about its demise, as the species was soon in great demand from the cage bird trade, and so was hunted close to extinction. In a double whammy, the development of Bali as a major tourist destination also led to the destruction of much of the bird's habitat.

Despite being Bali's national bird, by the 1990s there were just fifty individuals in the wild, a figure that has now risen to about a hundred. Ironically, however, the species' popularity as a cage bird means there are now more than 1,000 individuals in captivity, many of which are part of a breeding programme to release birds back to their original home.

Today, although the species is still classified by BirdLife International as Critically Endangered, it does appear to have turned a corner. Risks remain – not least continued poaching for the illegal cage bird trade in some areas – but hopefully the Bali starling will continue to delight local people and visitors to the island for the foreseeable future.

EPILOGUE

Their aerial evolutions before roosting are sufficiently remarkable, but perhaps still more so is the manner in which they leave the roosting-place in the morning.

Edmund Selous, *Bird Watching* (1901)

Another New Year's Day, but this time I've woken early, sober and keen to get out in the field to kick off my birding year. I'm back at the starling roost, at the RSPB's Ham Wall reserve, but this time I'm alone, rather than among a huge crowd.

That's because I've returned here to witness a spectacle that for me is just as special as the nightly murmurations: the daily departure of the birds at dawn. The great advantage is that I know where they went to roost last night, and so can position myself in exactly the right place to witness them leaving, just a stone's throw from where they are currently asleep.

The naturalist and writer Edmund Selous, who coined the phrase 'bird watching' as the title of his 1901 book was, like me, a devotee of this alternative early-morning spectacle:

This is not in one great body, as might have been expected, but in successive flights at intervals, each flight comprising, sometimes, hundreds of thousands of birds. Each of these great flights or uprushes takes place with startling suddenness, and it seems as though every individual bird composing it were linked to every other by some invisible material, as are knots on the meshes of a net by the visible twine connecting them.

And so, as I imagine Selous did over a century ago, I stand quietly as the first daylight of the new year seeps through the sky: at first just a glimmer of pale in the east, then a gradual lightening of the sky against the darker land beneath, and finally the soft orange sheen that foretells the rising of the sun. It dawns on me that although I rather enjoy the firework-display atmosphere of the evening events, sometimes I prefer to be on my own, able to respond to the birds without an accompanying human soundtrack of surprise and delight.

At first there is nothing to see, and nothing to hear apart from the song of a distant robin greeting the new day. Then, as my watch hand passes 7.45 a.m., half an hour before sunrise, I begin to hear something. To begin with, the calls are so soft I think I have imagined them, just a low murmur emanating from the heart of the reeds. But little by little the volume increases: a soft, bubbling chatter is soon a crescendo of sound, rather like the gradual rise in amplification of a human conversation as more and more people join in, raising their voices to be heard.

Moments later, and I see the first movement, as some of the birds climb to the fluffy tops of the reeds. A closer look at a single starling reveals the star-like markings on his feathers showing up well in the delicate morning light.

These reconnoitring birds are soon followed by a larger group rising a few feet into the air, pausing, then dropping back down again, as if uncertain whether they should take the plunge. Moments later a whooshing pulse of sound from their wingbeats reaches my ears, like rushing water.

Gradually, other groups of birds rise to the tops of the reeds. And then, as if on some unseen signal, a huge flock – thousands strong – takes to the wing, and begins to move away, still keeping only a few feet above the reed bed. As Selous noted, this happens without warning:

There is no preliminary, but at once a huge mass roars up from the still more immense multitude, as does a wave from the sea, or as a sudden cloud of dust is puffed by the wind from a dust heap.

Assailing my ears is what the wildlife sound recordist Gary Moore, who has also witnessed this scene many times, calls 'a wall of white noise'.

Like a speeded-up version of the previous evening's murmuration, but played in reverse, the flock heads away towards the horizon. This is a full-scale evacuation, all hesitation forgotten, as the birds go in search of food. Through my binoculars I try to follow them for as long as possible, the final birds only disappearing behind the distant landmark of Glastonbury Tor silhouetted to the east.

Did I really did witness the whole thing, or have I simply imagined it?

I walk back on my own – no chatting crowds, no excited children or eager dogs, just me – into the sounds and sights of a winter's morning: another plaintive robin, the madcap trilling of a wren and the explosive song of Cetti's warbler, as another new year begins.

Acknowledgements

No-one can even consider writing a book on the starling – or indeed starlings and mynas as a whole – without consulting the many works written by Dr Christopher Feare.

Chris began work on the European starling exactly half a century ago, in 1974, and has written several volumes on this species and the other members of its fascinating and diverse family – including *The Starling*, published in 1984, which is still highly relevant today. In recent years he has turned his attention and unrivalled expertise to help save globally threatened species of birds in the Seychelles from the invasive common myna. Chris has been characteristically generous in his help with my own book, and I owe him a huge debt of gratitude.

Other academics, friends and neighbours have also been very helpful: my thanks go to Professor Anne Goodenough for her advice on the science of starling murmurations; Dr Jessica Tipton of the Natural History Museum, for her evocative account of a starling roost at a Bracknell shopping centre; historian Dr Laura Sangha of the University of Exeter for drawing my attention to the fascinating story of 'the battle of the starlings', fought in the skies over Cork in October 1621; zoologist Walt Koenig, for drawing my attention to his fascinating paper on the ecological effects of starlings on native cavity-nesting birds; environmental humanists John MacNeill Miller (Allegheny College, Pennsylvania) and Lauren Fugate (Carnegie Mellon University,

Pennsylvania) for debunking the myth of how starlings were supposedly brought to North America; Sean Dooley from BirdLife Australia for providing information on starlings there; my former BBC colleague Chris Howard for describing the complex filming of the starling roost on Bodmin Moor; my dear friends Kate and Jerry Marwood for their excessively generous New Year's Eve hospitality; and my neighbour Rick Popham for telling me about the rural pastime of 'bird-batting'.

Special thanks to poets John Barlow and Rob Cowen (author of the book's epitaph, from his collection *The Heeding*), and the estate of the late Norman MacCaig, for permission to use extracts from their wonderful verse.

The very talented team at Square Peg (Penguin Random House) have done a great job on the book: Marianne Tatepo and Emily Martin in Editorial, Susie Merry in Publicity, Kate Reiners in the rights team; and the designers and production team, Amelia Tolley, Joe Howse and Lily Richards, who also found the lovely cover image from Lord Lilford's *Coloured Figures of the Birds of the British Islands*. Thanks, as ever, to my editor Graham Coster and my agent Broo Doherty.

And finally, a special thanks to my dear friends Kay and Graeme Mitchell, of Somerset Birdwatching Holidays, for allowing me, as their guide, to indulge in showing people the epic murmurations of starlings on the Somerset Levels.

List of Illustrations

p. 18 'Common Starling' from *A History of the Birds of Europe: including all the species inhabiting the western Palaearctic region* by Dresser, H. E. (Henry Eeles), 1838–1915, published by the author *c.*1871–81 © Biodiversity Heritage Library

p. 22 'Stubenvogel I' from *Meyers Konversations-Lexikon: Ein Nachschlagewerk des allgemeinen Wissens*, 5th edition, published by Bibliographisches Institut in Leipzig, 1895–97, chromalith illustration © ThePalmer / iStock

p. 23 (top) 'Common and Black Starling' from *The Royal Natural History: Volume 3* by Richard Lydekker, 1894–5 © Iconographic Archive / Alamy Stock Photo

p. 23 (bottom) 'Starling' from *The Handbook of British Birds: Volume 1* by H. F. Witherby, Rev F.C.R. Jourdain, Norman F. Ticehurst and Bernard W. Tucker, published by H. F. & G. Witherby Ltd in London, 1940

p. 26 'Vier Vogels' Anonymous print based on an original design by Adriaen Collaert, Amsterdam, 1659, print, © Rijksmuseum

p. 27 'Twee vogels in een landschap' by Adriaen Collaert, Amsterdam, 1598–1602, print, © Rijksmuseum

p. 31 'Rosy Starling "Sturnus roseus"' from *The Wellesley Albums 1798–1805*, watercolour, © British Library Archive / Bridgeman images

p. 32 'Rose-coloured Starling' from *The Handbook of British Birds: Volume 1* by H. F. Witherby, Rev F.C.R. Jourdain, Norman F. Ticehurst and Bernard W. Tucker, published by H. F. & G. Witherby Ltd in London, 1940

p. 36 'Starlings' by A. W. Seaby from *British Birds* by F. B. Kirkman, published in 1929

p. 37 'Peeps at Nature: Starlings' by Leslie Field Marchant, from *Treasure* n.303:2, November 1968, gouache on paper © Look and Learn / Bridgeman Images

p. 42 'Birds' from *Naturgeschichte des Tierreichs* (*Natural History of the*

Animal Kingdom), published by Emil Hänselmann, *c*.1885, colour lithograph © Purix Verlag Volker Christen / Bridgeman Images

p. 44 'Amydrus Tristram' from *The Survey of Western Palestine: The Fauna and Flora of Palestine* by Henry Baker Tristram, published by the Committee of the Palestine Exploration Fund, 1884 © Biodiversity Heritage Library

p. 46 'Starling. Sturnus vulgaris, Linn. Winter' by John Gerrard Keulemans from *Coloured figures of the Birds of the British Islands* published by R. H. Porter, London, 1885–97, colour lithograph © Biodiversity Heritage Library

p. 52 'Kalenderblad januari met spreeuwen' by Theo van Hoytema in The Hague, Amsterdam, 1913, print © Rijksmuseum

p. 53 'Happy Pentecost' postcard from Germany, *c*.1925 © Interfoto / Alamy Stock Photo

p. 55 'Branwen tames a starling' by Talbot Hughes, from *Land of My Fathers*, published by Hodder and Stoughton *c*.1915, colour lithograph © Bridgeman Images

p. 57 'Kalenderblad februari met spreeuw' by Theo van Hoytema, published by Hilyersum in Amsterdam, 1901, print © Rijksmuseum

p. 60 'Passeres, Larks' from *The Natural History of the Animal Kingdom for the Use of Young People, Part II: Birds* by W. F. Kirby, 1889, colour lithograph © Look and Learn / Bridgeman Images

p. 61 'Nesting Starlings' *c*.1893, engraving © Sunny Celeste / Alamy Stock Photo

p. 65 'European Starling', drawing © NPL – DeA Picture Library / Bridgeman Images

p. 66 'Sturnus vulgaris. The common starling' by O. Milano Dressler, from *Natural History of Birds that Nest in Lombardy*, 1865 © British Library / Bridgeman Images

p. 68 'Peeps at Nature: Starlings' by Leslie Field Marchant, from

Treasure n.303:2, November 1968, gouache on paper © Look and Learn / Bridgeman Images

p. 70 'Sturnus vulgaris' from *The Birds of Great Britain* by John Gould, 1873, coloured lithograph © Natural History Museum, London / Bridgeman Images

p. 74 'Eggs' from *British Birds* by F. B. Kirkman, published in 1929

p. 75 'European starling (Sturnus vulgaris) bringing food to young in the nest' © NPL – DeA Picture Library / Bridgeman Images

p. 84 'A starling sitting on a stone in front of a church' by Josiah Wood Whymper, 1813–1903 (coloured wood engraving) © Wellcome collection

p. 89 'Twee grijze spreeuwen' by Ohara Koson, 1900–36, colour woodcut © Rijksmuseum

p. 90 'Sturnus vulgaris. Gemeiner Star. The common starling' from *Naturgeschichte der Vogel Mittel-Europas* by Johann Andreas Naumann, 1905 © British Library / Bridgeman Images

p. 96 'The common starling, Sturnus vulgaris, also known as the European starling' © Falkensteinfoto / Alamy Stock Photo

p. 100 'Hunting net in the Rhine River' from *L'Illustration Journal Universel*, Paris, 1860, engraving © Oldtime / Alamy Stock Photo

p. 106 'a pair of Starlings eating berries from a tree', 1870, engraving © duncan1890 / iStock

p. 112 'The starling' from *A Natural History of Birds* by Eleazar Albin, 1738, coloured lithograph © British Library / Bridgeman Images

p. 115 'A very large flock of starlings (known as a murmuration) flying together at dusk over a small area of woodland in England, during winter' by George Clerk, 6 July 2018, photograph © Georgeclerk / istock

p. 122 'Kalenderblad voor februari 1907 met spreeuwen' by Theo van

Hoytema, printed by Tresling & Comp, Amsterdam, 1906, colour print © Rijksmuseum

p. 124 'Birds: Passeriformes' © NPL – DeA Picture Library / Bridgeman Images

p. 126 'Kalenderblad maart met spreeuwen en eenden' by Theo van Hoytema, printed by Tresling & Comp in The Hague, 1911 © Rijksmuseum

p. 130 'Common Starling' by Magnus Wright and Wilhelm von Wright from *Fåglar efter Naturen och på sten ritade* by Magnus, Wilhelm and Ferdinand von Wright, published by Förlaget Svenska Fåglar Stockholm, 1927, colour lithograph © Purix Verlag Volker Christen / Bridgeman Images

p. 134 'Plein te Cork waar de bewoners kijken naar de duizenden spreeuwen in de lucht' by Jan Luyken, published by Pieter van der Aa, Leiden, Amsterdam, 1698, engraving © Rijksmuseum

p. 135 'Jacht op kraaien en spreeuwen' by Jan Collaert after design by Jan van der Straet, published by Philips Galle, Antwerp 1594–98, engraving © Rijksmuseum

p. 142 'Murmuration photo' by Mike Dabell, UK, photograph © mike-dabell / istock

p. 144 'Sednine: Starling' from a series of advertising cards issued by Allen & Hanbury's advertising Sednine, 1966 © Wellcome Collection

p. 146 'The Aeroplane' by Alfred Stieglitz, October 1911, photogravure © Museum of Fine Arts, Houston / The Target Collection of American Photography, museum purchase funded by Target Stores / Bridgeman Images

p. 148 'Spreeuwen in de regen' by Ohara Koson, published by Matsuki Keikichi, Tokyo, Japan, 1900–30, colour woodcut © Rijksmuseum

p. 157 'Starling' from *Coloured Figures of the Birds of the British Islands* by